D1394879

The Mitchell Beazley
pocket guide to
Wild Flowers
Peter D. Moore Ph.D.

Mitchell Beazley

Nomenclature

The common names of wild flowers vary widely and are often misleading, but the scientific (Latin) name is determined by strict international rules. Every plant has a double name: the first is the genus name, the second the species (specific) name. Thus Lords and ladies or Cuckoo pint is always given the Latin name *Arum maculatum*. Each genus contains one or more species; several related genera are grouped into a family—*Arum* is in the family Araceae. A species may be divided into subspecies showing a small variation and have a third name: e.g. the bog orchid is *Orchis laxiflora* subsp *palustris*. This book follows the Latin names used in the standard work *Flora Europaea* (see p. 192).

Abbreviations

alt	alternate	hrlss	hairless	seg	segment
ann	annual	Ht	height	sev	several
bi	biennial	inc	including	sh	shoot
br	branch	indiv	individual	sim	similar
c.	about	infl	inflorescence	sol	solitary
cm	centimetre	lf(y)	leaf(y)	sp(p)	species (plural)
col	colour	lflt	leaflet	spl	sepal
D	distribution	lvs	leaves	stk(d)	stalk(ed)
decid	deciduous	m	metre	stm	stamen
diam	diameter	mm	millimetre	str	structure
esp	especially	mts	mountains	subsp	subspecies
fl	flower	nr	near	succ	succulent
Fl	flowering season	opp	opposite	unstkd	unstalked
fr	fruit	per	perennial	uprt	upright
frag	fragrant	pr(d)	pair(ed)	v	very
gp	group	ptl	petal	veg	vegetative
hr(y)	hair(y)	rt	root	yr	year
♂ male	♀ female	1–12	months of the year January–December		

Distribution (D) throughout Europe

Arct	Arctic	NE	Northeastern (E Baltic–Finland)
C	Central (E France–Poland)	NW	Northwestern (Britain–Scandinavia)
Carp	Carpathians	Nwy	Norway
Dk	Denmark	S	Southern (France–S Germany)
E	Eastern (E Germany–E Baltic)	SE	Southeastern (S Germany–Czechoslovakia)
EC	East Central (E Germany–Poland)	SW	Southwestern (France–SW Britain)
Eng	England	Swed	Sweden
Eur	Europe	T	Throughout
Fenno-scand	Fennoscandinavia (Scandinavia–Finland	UK	United Kingdom
Fin	Finland	W	Western (Britain–France–W Scandinavia)
GB	Great Britain		
Med	Mediterranean		
N	Northern (N Britain–Denmark–Fennoscandinavia)		

Editor Ruth Binney **Executive Editor** Susannah Read
Designer Derek St Romaine **Art Editor** Douglas Wilson
Production Julian Deeming

Illustrators Jac Jones/The Garden Studio; Josephine Martin/
The Garden Studio; Nina Roberts/The Garden
Studio; Kathleen Smith; Gill Tomblin

Edited and designed by
Mitchell Beazley International Ltd
Michelin House, 81 Fulham Road, London SW3 6RB
© Mitchell Beazley International Ltd 1980
Reprinted 1981, 1982, 1983, 1984, 1986, 1988, 1990, 1991, 1992, 1993, 1995
ISBN 0 85533 268 9
Typeset by Tradespools Ltd. Frome
Colour reproduction by Photoprint Plates Ltd
Produced by Mandarin Offset
Printed and bound in Malaysia

Contents

Introduction

The sheer beauty of wild flowers needs no emphasis, yet their enjoyment can be greatly enhanced when spiced with more understanding of their construction and relations to one another. Fundamental to this fuller knowledge is correct identification and it is here that we seek to meet the naturalist's needs.

One valuable feature of plants is their immobility—but this also makes them vulnerable for they are easily destroyed by careless misuse. This book is designed so that it can easily be carried into the field for on-the-spot identification, making it unnecessary to collect specimens and so deplete the countryside of its natural heritage. The serious field botanist will also need a hand lens (× 10 is the ideal magnification) and a notebook. Sometimes it may be necessary to remove a single flower (but *only* if the plant is widespread) to look at it in detail by cutting a section through it, so take a pocket scalpel with you.

Over 1,000 European wild flower species are illustrated in this book, and others are mentioned in the text. The selection of plants has been based on their frequency and ease of identification; some have been omitted because their special features are too complex. Geographically the book covers N Europe, south to the Massif Central in France and east to the Soviet Union. The many lovely plants exclusive to the Alps and the Mediterranean are not here as they are too numerous to deal with fully.

How to use this book

The best way to begin identifying a wild flower is to keep this book closed and examine the plant! It may be tempting to flick through the pictures but this is not the most effective and not necessarily the quickest way to achieve accurate identification.

Start with the whole plant. What size is it? Is it erect, creeping or tussock-forming? How are its leaves arranged? What shape and size are they? Are they stalked or hairy? Are the stem leaves different from those at the base? Are the flowers arranged singly or in groups? Now look more closely at the flower and examine a single one in detail (the explanations on pages 4–6 show plant parts and the ways they can be arranged). How many sepals and petals has it? Are they joined or completely free from one another? Are the sepals hairy? What colour are the petals? How many stamens are there? Are they attached to the petals or to the base of the flower? Now examine the carpels. This may be more difficult for they are often fused in a group—if so, are their styles and stigmas free? It may be helpful to cut a section across the ovary to count the number of cells inside, but let common sense be your guide. Finally note the type of habitat in which the plant is growing, e.g. heathland, roadside or grassland, and any obvious environmental features such as damp or chalky soil.

With all this information you should now be able to tackle the key to plant families on pages 6–11; then turn to the pages dealing with the family to which the plant belongs and check against the pictures and descriptions of key features of each species. Do not rely on the illustrations alone; always check that the plant also matches with its "word picture".

Alongside the Latin and English common names of each plant are symbols showing the habitat in which it is most likely to be growing. These are explained on the next page. Because plant heights are very variable an average figure is given; the same is true for some plant parts. Unless stated, the measurement refers to the length of the part concerned. To save space abbreviations have been used (see opposite). Technical terms have been kept to a minimum but those used are explained on pp. 4–5.

Habitat symbols

Woods, forests, grassland

Coniferous woods

Deciduous woods

Grassland, meadows

Chalk and limestone grassland

Mountain, moorland

Mountain grassland

Mountain rocks, scree

Heath, moorland

Freshwater

Marsh and fens

Bogs

Aquatic

Banks, edges

Salt marsh

Disturbed ground

Wasteland, arable

Hedges, scrub

Roadsides

Walls

Maritime

Sand dunes

Shingle

Cliffs

Near sea

Sea

Soils

Damp soil

Acid soil

Chalky soil

Sandy soil

Glossary

Alternate

Axil

Bracteole

Bract

Elliptic

Compound

Leaflet

Ligule

Ray floret

Inferior

Above towards the top of a plant or plant part; upper surface of a leaf

Achene one-seeded dry fruit that does not split

Alternate (alt) leaves growing singly at nodes on either side of a stem

Anther pollen-producing organ, top part of a stamen

Axil the angle between a stem and a leaf or bract

Axillary growing in an axil

Basal nearest the ground

Below towards the base of a plant or plant part; lower surface of a leaf

Biennial (bi) plant taking more than one but less than two years to complete its life cycle

Bifid, bifurcating forked into two

Bloom powdery or waxy covering

Bract leaf-like structure with a flower in its axil or, in Compositae (daisy family), in a whorl round flower head

Bracteole a secondary bract usually on the flower stalk or, in Umbelliferae (carrot family) bract-like structure at the base of a secondary umbel

Bulbil small bulb found in leaf axils or among flowers

Capsule dry fruit that splits open when ripe

Carpel single female unit of a flower consisting of the stigma, style and ovary (see p 6)

Cell seed-containing cavity in an ovary, best seen by cutting ovary horizontally

Compound in several parts, as a leaf divided into leaflets

Corm swollen underground stem

Elliptic oval and narrowed at the ends

Emergent part of an aquatic plant growing above water

Entire not divided—without teeth or lobes

Epicalyx extra sepal ring outside true sepals

Equal the same length

Floret one of the small flowers in a composite (e.g. daisy); disc florets are tubular, ray florets strap-shaped

Follicle dry fruit that splits down one side only

Glaucous blue-grey in colour, covered with a bloom

Head compact mass of flowers or florets

Helmet hooded upper lobe of an orchid flower

Herb plant normally without woody tissue

Inferior an ovary placed below other plant parts

Inflorescence (infl) grouping of individual flowers

Keel lower petals of a leguminous flower (e.g. pea) or a sharp ridge on a plant part (see p 6)

4

Lance-shaped in the shape of a spear

Lateral placed at the side

Leaflet (lflt) leaf-like structure, part of a compound leaf

Ligulate possessing a tongue-like projection (ligule)

Linear long and narrow with parallel sides

Lip lobe of a flower in which petals are fused

Lobed divided into (usually round) segments

Midrib central vein of a leaf

Node site on a stem at which a leaf or leaves arise

Nut woody, single-seeded fruit

Obovate egg-shaped (ovate) but wider towards the tip

Ochreae sheathing leaf bases in Polygonaceae (docks)

Opposite (opp) two leaves at a node on opposite sides of a stem and in the same plane

Ovary flower part containing structures that develop into seeds. Part of one or several fused carpels (see p 6)

Ovoid egg-shaped

Palmate divided as the palm and fingers of a hand

Pappus simple or feathery hairs in fruit and flowers of the Compositae (daisy family)

Parasite plant dependent on other plants as a food source, normally with no green pigment. Partial or semi-parasites may have green pigments

Perennial (per) plant surviving for more than two years

Pinnate leaf divided into leaflets arranged on opposite sides of the midrib; 2-pinnate: each leaflet is further subdivided in a pinnate way; 3-pinnate: 3 levels of subdivision

Radially symmetrical symmetrical about more than one axis passing through the centre

Reflexed bent backwards

Rhizome creeping underground stem bearing roots, leafy and flowering shoots. An organ of propagation

Rootstock underground stem from which new plant parts arise

Runner long slim prostrate shoot, rooting to form a new plant at its tip or elsewhere along its length

Scale thin flap, often a modified leaf

Scape flower stem growing directly from the base of a plant as in Primulaceae (primroses), lacking leaves

Sepals (spls) outer ring of flower parts outside the petals

Serrate with a toothed edge

Sessile without a stalk

Simple not divided or lobed

Solitary (sol) flower not associated with other flowers in a head or inflorescence

Spadix elongated club-like flower head

Spathe leaf-like bract or sheath enclosing a flower head

Spathulate spoon-shaped (narrow at the base)

Spike long unbranched flower heads bearing unstalked flowers, the youngest flowers at the tip

Spur hollow projection from a petal or sepal

Stamen (stm) male organ of a flower made up of anthers each borne on a stalk or filament (see p 6)

Standard upright rear petal as in a pea flower (see p 6)

Stigma tip of the style on which pollen is deposited

Stipule leaf-like or scale-like outgrowth at the base of a leaf stalk; usually in pairs

Stolon shoot growing from a plant above or below ground; gives rise to a new plant at its tip

Style elongated structure joining the stigma and ovary

Superior ovary with other flower parts attached beneath

Tendril coiled organ on stem or leaf, used for climbing

Terminal at the apex of a plant or plant part

Trifoliate with three leaflets

Tuber swollen underground stem or root

Umbel flower head with flower stalks arising from one point and spread out like umbrella spokes. Smaller (secondary) umbels often arise from main umbel stalks

Whorl 3 or more leaves radiating from a single point

Wing expanded ridge, e.g., on a stem or fruit; one of the side petals on leguminous (pea family) (see p 6)

Lance-shaped

Linear

Obovate

Opposite

Node

Ovoid

Palmate

2-pinnate

Serrate

Simple

Spathulate

Stipule

Umbel

Whorl

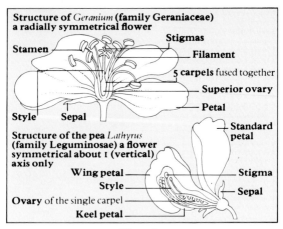

Structure of *Geranium* **(family Geraniaceae) a radially symmetrical flower**

Stigmas
Stamen
Filament
5 carpels fused together
Superior ovary
Petal
Style   Sepal

Structure of the pea *Lathyrus* **(family Leguminosae) a flower symmetrical about 1 (vertical) axis only**

Standard petal
Wing petal
Stigma
Style
Sepal
Ovary of the single carpel
Keel petal

Plant key

Work the key by asking questions; each offers 2 (rarely 3) choices between which you should choose on the basis of your observations (see p. 3). The plant shown here is a test example; it is an erect herb about 50 cm tall with yellow flowers found growing in wet grassland.

Superior ovary
Styles
Stamens
Sepal

Horizontal section through 3 fused carpels

The first decision to make from the key is between options **1a** and **1b**, i.e., whether the plant is green or not. The plant is green so go to **2**; it is terrestrial so you proceed to **4**. Now you are asked about the flowers. They are obvious and coloured so you are sent to **5**; there are exactly 5 petals so you choose **5a** and are directed to **6** where you must choose option **6a**. This leads to **7**. Now a careful check is needed to see if the 5 petals are joined in a tube (even if only near the base). The plant has free (unjoined) petals so you go on to **8** which concerns the shape of the flower. Because the plant has more than one plane of symmetry (i.e., is radially symmetrical), unlike a pea flower, for example, you arrive at **GROUP H**.

GROUP H (p.9) begins with 3 options, all demanding detailed examination of the ovary. In this plant the flower parts (petals, sepals and stamens) are attached below the ovary so the ovary is superior. There is a single ovary with 3 styles projecting so this suggests 3 carpels. A horizontal section cut through the ovary confirms this so you choose **1b** and move to **6**. The plant has many—certainly far more than 10—stamens so go to **7**. Leaves are in opposite pairs, stipules are absent, so the choice is **7b** which leads to **9**. As already shown there are 3 free styles, suggesting that **9b** is the correct choice. A careful look at the stamens shows them to be joined in groups near their bases, which confirms that the plant is a member of the **Guttiferae** or St John's wort family (pp. 76–77).

Turning to these pages, you will see that members of the Guttiferae vary in such features as growth habit, flower size, hairiness and stem character. Our plant is hairless and has square stems, which confirms it as *Hypericum tetrapterum*, the Square-stemmed St John's wort.

Key to plant groups	**Proceed to**
1a Plants with no green parts	**Group A** (below)
1b Plants green	**2**
2a Growing in water	**3**
2b Growing on land	**4**
3a Floating aquatics, rooted in mud	**Group B** (below)
3b Aquatics, rooted in mud	**Group C** (below)
4a Individual flowers inconspicuous, may be in clusters, e.g., catkins, colour green or brown	**Group D** (p. 8)
4b Flowers obvious, coloured	**5**
5a 5 or more petals or petal-like parts	**6**
5b Fewer than 5 petals	**10**
6a 5 petals	**7**
6b 6 or more petals	**Group L** (p. 11)
7a Petals free (not joined together)	**8**
7b Petals joined together	**9**
8a Flowers radially symmetrical	**Group H** (p. 9)
8b Flowers symmetrical about 1 axis only	**Group J** (p. 10)
9a Flowers radially symmetrical	**Group I** (p. 10)
9b Flowers symmetrical about 1 axis only, hooded, lipped or spurred	**Group K** (p.11)
10a 0, 2 or 3 petals or petal-like parts	**Group E** (p. 8)
10b 4 petals	**11**
11a Petals free	**Group F** (p. 8)
11b Petals joined at least at base	**Group G** (p. 9)

Group A Plants with no green pigment

1a Plant erect	**2**
1b Plant twining around another species	**Convolvulaceae p. 105**
2a Flowers radially symmetrical drooping	**Pyrolaceae p. 92**
2b Flowers not radially symmetrical	**3**
3a Flowers 2-lipped, tubular below	**Orobanchaceae p. 128**
3b 6 free petal-like structures, prominent lower lip	**Orchidaceae p. 170**

Group B Floating aquatics, not rooted in mud

1a Plant small (less than 1 cm), disc-like or lobed	**Lemnaceae p. 181**
1b Plant larger than 1 cm, not disc-like	**2**
2a Leaves finely divided, has small bladders	**Lentibulariaceae** (*Utricularia*) p. 129
2b Leaves not divided	**3**
3a Flowers with 4 petals	**Trapaceae p. 80**
3b Flowers with 3 petals	**Hydrocharitaceae p. 157**

Group C Aquatic plants, rooted in mud

1a Plant erect, tall, emerging from water	**2**
1b Plant not erect, usually immersed or floating	**7**
2a Flowers conspicuous, individual flowers greater than 1 cm	**Butomaceae p. 157** **Alismataceae p. 156**
2b Individual flowers small, inconspicuous, but may be in dense, obvious clusters	**3**
3a Leaves whorled	**Hippuridaceae p. 83**
3b Leaves not whorled	**4**
4a Inflorescence surrounded by a sheath (spathe)	**Araceae** (*Calla*) p. 180
4b Inflorescence without encircling sheath	**5**
5a Inflorescence cylindrical	**6**
5b Inflorescence globular, fruits pointed	**Sparganiaceae p. 181**
6a Plant sweet-smelling, inflorescence to one side	**Araceae** (*Acorus*) p. 180
6b Plant not scented, inflorescence terminal	**Typhaceae p. 181**
7a Flowers conspicuous, white or yellow	**8**
7b Flowers inconspicuous, but may be in dense spikes, green or brown	**10**
8a Petals free	**Nymphaceae p. 27**
8b Petals united	**9**

Group C continued

9a	Flowers radially symmetrical, white	**Menyanthaceae p. 102**
9b	Flowers symmetrical about only 1 axis, yellow	**Lentibulariaceae** (*Utricularia*) **p. 129**
10a	Leaves whorled	**Ceratophyllaceae p. 28** **Haloragaceae p. 83** **Najadaceae p. 159**
10b	Lower leaves in opposite pairs	**Callitrichaceae p. 109** **Najadaceae p. 159** **Potamogetonaceae** (*Groenlandia*) **p. 158**
10c	Lower leaves alternate	**Zosteraceae p. 158** **Potamogetonaceae p. 158** **Ruppiaceae p. 159**

Group D Terrestrial plants. Flowers inconspicuous, green or brown, but often arranged in prominent clusters

1a	Flowers in catkin-like structures	2
1b	Flowers not in catkins	3
2a	Erect or creeping shrubs	**Salicaceae p. 12** **Myricaceae p. 12**
2b	Erect herbs or climbers	**Urticaceae p. 13** **Cannabaceae p. 13**
3a	Plant parasitic on trees	**Loranthaceae p. 14**
3b	Plant not parasitic on trees	4
4a	Leaves compound	5
4b	Leaves simple	8
4c	Leaves absent, stems cylindrical, succulent	**Chenopodiaceae** (*Salicornia*) **p. 19**
5a	Flowers in dense heads	6
5b	Flowers not in dense heads	7
6a	Flowers in heads of 5, flowers at right angles to each other	**Adoxaceae p. 131**
6b	More than 5 flowers per head	**Rosaceae p. 50**
7a	No petals, 4 stamens	**Rosaceae** (*Alchemilla*) **p. 54** (*Aphanes*) **p. 55** **Ranunculaceae** (*Thalictrum*) **p. 34**
7b	4–5 petals, many stamens	
8a	Inflorescence a dense spike with sheath (spathe)	**Araceae p. 180**
8b	Not so	9
9a	Milky juice, flowers in umbels	**Euphorbiaceae p. 71**
9b	No milky juice present, flowers not arranged in umbels	10
10a	Opposite or whorled leaves	11
10b	Alternate leaves	14
11a	Low, creeping stems	12
11b	Plant erect	13
12a	5 sepals and petals	**Caryophyllaceae p. 20**
12b	4 sepals	**Saxifragaceae** (*Chrysosplenium*) **p. 49**
13a	Stinging hairs, 4 stamens	**Urticaceae p. 13**
13b	No stinging hairs, many stamens	**Euphorbiaceae** (*Mercurialis*) **p. 72**
14a	Leaves with sheaths around base	**Polygonaceae p. 15**
14b	No sheaths at leaf bases	15
15a	Flowers in dense, narrow spikes, leaves linear, not fleshy	**Plantaginaceae p. 130** **Ranunculaceae** (*Myosurus*) **p. 34**
15b	Flowers not in narrow spikes, often fleshy and/or mealy	**Chenopodiaceae p. 18**

Group E Terrestrial plants. Flowers conspicuous, 0, 2 or 3 petals

1a	Petals absent, flowers in dense, reddish heads	**Rosaceae** (*Sanguisorba*) **p. 55**
1b	Petals present, flowers not in dense heads	2
2a	2 petals	**Onagraceae** (*Circaea*) **p. 81**
2b	3 petals	3
3a	Petals joined in a tube	**Aristolochiaceae p. 14**
3b	Petals free	**Alismataceae p. 156**

Group F Terrestrial plants. Flowers conspicuous, 4 petals or petal-like parts, not joined together at base nor in a tube

1a	Leaves undivided	**2**
1b	Leaves divided into segments	**7**
2a	More than 8 stamens	**Resedaceae p. 44**
2b	Less than 8 stamens	**3**
3a	4 sepals	**4**
3b	2 sepals, soon falling	**Papaveraceae p. 35**
4a	Ovary inferior	**5**
4b	Ovary superior	**6**
5a	Flowers with large, whitish, petal-like bracts	**Cornaceae p. 83**
5b	Flowers with true petals	**Onagraceae p. 80**
6a	Ovary 1-celled	**Caryophyllaceae p. 20**
6b	Ovary 2-celled	**Cruciferae p. 36**
6c	Ovary 5- or 6-celled	**Linaceae (*Radiola*) p. 70**
7a	More than 8 stamens, leaves palmate-lobed	**Rosaceae (*Potentilla erecta*) p. 52**
7b	Usually 6 stamens, leaves not palmate	**Cruciferae p. 36**

Group G Terrestrial plants. Flowers conspicuous, 4 petals or petal-like parts, joined together at their base, or in a tube

1a	Flowers radially symmetrical	**2**
1b	Flowers not radially symmetrical	**6**
2a	Leaves in whorls	**3**
2b	Leaves not in whorls	**4**
3a	4 or 5 stamens	**Rubiaceae p. 103**
3b	8 stamens	**Ericaceae p. 93**
4a	Leaves opposite, 5 stamens	**Gentianaceae p. 99**
4b	Leaves alternate, more than 5 stamens	**5**
5a	Sepals petal-like, no true petals	**Thymelaeaceae p. 76**
5b	Green sepals and coloured petals present	**Ericaceae p. 93**
6a	Flowers in dense heads, whorled bracts beneath	**Dipsacaceae p. 133**
6b	Flowers not in dense heads	**7**
7a	2 stamens, ovary 1-celled	**Papaveraceae (*Fumaria*) p. 36**
7b	4 stamens, ovary 2-celled	**Scrophulariaceae p. 118**

Group H Terrestrial plants. Flowers conspicuous, 5 petals or petal-like parts, not joined together

1a	Ovary superior, carpels free	**2**
1b	Ovary superior, carpels fused	**6**
1c	Ovary inferior	**21**
2a	More than 10 stamens	**3**
2b	10 or fewer stamens	**4**
3a	Stipules present	**Rosaceae p. 50**
3b	Stipules absent	**Ranunculaceae p. 28**
4a	Succulent (fleshy) leaves	**Crassulaceae p. 46**
4b	Leaves not succulent	**5**
5a	Leaves divided into lobes	**Rutaceae p. 73, Rosaceae (*Sibbaldia*) p. 53**
5b	Leaves not divided into lobes	**Polygonaceae p. 15, Ranunculaceae (*Myosurus*) p. 34**
6a	More than 10 stamens	**7**
6b	10 or fewer stamens	**10**
7a	Leaves alternate, stipules present	**8**
7b	Leaves opposite, no stipules	**9**
8a	Leaves palmate, stamens fused in a ring	**Malvaceae p. 75**
8b	Leaves not palmately lobed, stamens free	**Rosaceae p. 50**
9a	Single style, stamens free	**Cistaceae p. 79**
9b	Several styles, stamens in bundles	**Guttiferae p. 76**
10a	2 sepals	**Portulacaceae p. 20**
10b	More than 2 sepals	**11**
11a	Leaves opposite or whorled	**12**
11b	Leaves alternate or in a basal rosette	**14**
12a	Leaves simple, unlobed	**13**
12b	Leaves palmately or pinnately lobed	**Geraniaceae p. 68**
13a	Ovary 1-celled	**Caryophyllaceae p. 20, Frankeniaceae p. 82**

Group H continued

13b	Ovary 4–5 celled	**Linaceae p. 70**
14a	Leaves with sticky glands, insectivorous	**Droseraceae p. 45**
14b	Not so	**15**
15a	Leaves with 3 lobes	**Oxalidaceae p. 67**
15b	Not so	**16**
16a	5 stigmas	**17**
16b	Fewer than 5 stigmas	**19**
17a	Leaves entire (not lobed)	**18**
17b	Leaves pinnate or palmately lobed	**Geraniaceae p. 68**
18a	Many stem leaves present	**Linaceae p. 70**
18b	Leaves confined to basal rosette	**Plumbaginaceae p. 99**
19a	1 style	**Pyrolaceae p. 92**
19b	2–4 styles	**20**
20a	5 stamens alternating with feathery structures	**Parnassiaceae p. 50**
20b	10 stamens	**Saxifragaceae p. 48**
21a	More than 5 stamens	**22**
21b	5 stamens, flowers in umbels	**23**
22a	More than 10 stamens	**Rosaceae p. 50**
22b	10 stamens	**Saxifragaceae p. 48**
23a	Herbs	**Umbelliferae p. 84**
23b	Woody climber	**Araliaceae p. 84**

Group I Terrestrial plants. Flowers conspicuous, 5 petals joined together, radially symmetrical

1a	Ovary superior	**2**
1b	Ovary inferior	**12**
2a	10 stamens	**3**
2b	5 stamens	**5**
3a	Woody plants, usually evergreen	**Ericaceae p. 93**
3b	Succulent, round-leaved herb	**Crassulaceae (*Umbilicus*) p. 47**
4a	Stamens opposite the petals	**5**
4b	Stamens alternating with the petals	**6**
5a	Single stigma and style	**Primulaceae p. 96**
5b	5 stigmas	**Plumbaginaceae p. 99**
6a	Leaves opposite	**7**
6b	Leaves alternate	**8**
7a	2 free carpels with a single style	**Apocynaceae p. 102**
7b	Single ovary with 2 styles or 1 style, 2 stigmas	**Gentianaceae p. 99**
7c	Single ovary and style, 3-lobed stigma	**Diapensiaceae p. 91**
8a	Ovary strongly 4-lobed	**Boraginaceae p. 106**
8b	Not so	**9**
9a	Flowers in a terminal inflorescence	**10**
9b	Flowers axillary or in axillary clusters	**11**
10a	Leaves simple	**Scrophulariaceae p. 118**
10b	Leaves pinnate	**Polemoniaceae p. 105**
11a	Sepals free	**Convolvulaceae p. 105**
11b	Sepals united in a tube	**Solanaceae p. 117**
12a	8–10 stamens	**Ericaceae p. 93**
12b	5 or fewer stamens	**13**
13a	Flowers in dense heads	**14**
13b	Flowers not in dense heads	**16**
14a	Stamens completely free	**15**
14b	Stamens united by their anthers into a tube	**Compositae p. 137**
15a	5 stamens, alternate leaves	**Campanulaceae p. 134**
15b	2 or 4 stamens, opposite leaves	**Dipsacaceae p. 133**
16a	Leaves opposite	**17**
16b	Leaves alternate	**19**
17a	Creeping with flowers in pairs	**Caprifoliaceae (*Linnaea*) p. 132**
17b	Erect, with small flowers in clusters	**18**
18a	Milky sap, ovary with 2 carpels, 2-celled	**Asclepiadaceae p. 102**
18b	No milky sap, single-celled ovary	**Valerianaceae p. 132**
19a	Twining climber	**Cucurbitaceae p. 82**
19b	Not climbing	**Campanulaceae p. 134, Primulaceae (*Samolus*) p. 98**

Group J Terrestrial plants. Flowers conspicuous, 5 free petals, but flowers symmetrical about only 1 axis

1a	More than 8 stamens	**2**
1b	8 or fewer stamens	**3**
2a	10 stamens, no spur to flower	**Leguminosae p. 56**
2b	Many stamens, flowers spurred	**Ranunculaceae p. 28**
3a	5 stamens, flowers spurred	**Violaceae p. 78**
3b	8 stamens, flowers not spurred	**Polygalaceae p. 73**

Group K Terrestrial plants. Flowers conspicuous, 5 joined petals, flowers hooded, lipped or spurred, symmetrical about 1 axis

1a	Flowers in dense heads	**2**
1b	Flowers not in dense heads	**3**
2a	Leaves opposite	**Dipsacaceae p. 133**
2b	Leaves alternate	**Globulariaceae p. 128**
3a	Flowers spurred	**4**
3b	Flowers not spurred	**5**
4a	Sticky, insectivorous leaves in rosette	**Lentibulariaceae p. 129**
4b	Leaves not sticky, present on fleshy stem	**Balsaminaceae p. 74**
5a	Stamens joined in a tube by their anthers	**Campanulaceae (*Lobelia*) p. 136**
5b	Stamens free	**6**
6a	Woody, twining climber, 5 stamens	**Caprifoliaceae p. 132**
6b	Not a climber, 2 or 4 stamens	**7**
7a	Ovary 2-celled	**Scrophulariaceae p. 118**
7b	Ovary 4-celled	**Labiatae p. 110, Verbenaceae p. 109**

Group L Terrestrial plants. Flowers conspicuous, 6 or more petals or petal-like parts

1a	Petals free	**2**
1b	Petals joined together	**13**
2a	More than 12 stamens	**3**
2b	12 or fewer stamens	**4**
3a	Stipules present, clear area round ovary	**Rosaceae p. 50**
3b	Stipules absent, no clear area round ovary	**Ranunculaceae p. 28**
4a	Ovary superior	**5**
4b	Ovary inferior	**10**
5a	3 stamens (may be joined together)	**6**
5b	More than 3 stamens	**7**
6a	Leaves linear, flowers stalked in leaf axils	**Empetraceae p. 95**
6b	Leaves broad, pointed, stiff, flowers stalked in centre of leaf-like structure	**Liliaceae (*Ruscus*) p. 166**
7a	Leaves with sticky glands (insectivorous) all in basal rosette	**Droseraceae p. 45**
7b	Leaves without sticky glands	**8**
8a	Leaves cylindrical, succulent	**Crassulaceae p. 46**
8b	Leaves not succulent	**9**
9a	2 whorls of 3 petal-like parts, no green sepals	**Liliaceae p. 159**
9b	Single whorl of petals, sepals green	**10**
10a	Flowers pink or red	**Lythraceae p. 82**
10b	Flowers yellow/green or white	**Resedaceae p. 44**
11a	Flowers radially symmetrical	**12**
11b	Flowers symmetrical about only one axis	**Orchidaceae p. 170**
12a	6 stamens	**Amaryllidaceae p. 167**
12b	3 stamens	**Iridaceae p. 168**
13a	Climber with heart-shaped leaves	**Dioscoreaceae p. 169**
13b	Not a climber	**14**
14a	No obvious sepals or sepals petal-like	**15**
14b	Green, leafy sepals present	**18**
15a	Flowers in dense heads, surrounded by whorls of bracts	**Compositae p. 137**
15b	Flowers not so arranged	**16**
16a	Ovary superior	**Liliaceae p. 159**
16b	Ovary inferior	**17**
17a	6 stamens	**Amaryllidaceae p. 167**
17b	3 stamens	**Iridaceae p. 168**
18a	Stamens opposite petal lobes	**Primulaceae p. 96**
18b	Stamens alternating with petal lobes	**Gentianaceae p. 99**

Willow family Salicaceae

Deciduous trees and shrubs with simple leaves that often have outgrowths (stipules) at their base. Male and female flowers without sepals or petals are in catkins on separate plants.

Dwarf willow	Creeping willow
Salix herbacea	*S. repens*

Lvs untoothed, with silky hrs

Lvs glossy above, veins prominent

Catkins on short shs

♂ *catkins* slender, to 2 cm long

Creeping stems can stabilize sand dunes

Prostrate shrub. Shoots rise only 2–3 cm above soil surface. Lvs to 2 cm, rounded, edges toothed *D:* Fennoscand, Carpathians; *Fl:* 4–5

Perennial. Creeping stems and uprt shs to 1.5 m. Lvs to 4.5 cm and longer than broad appear before catkins. *D:* N to S. Scand; *Fl:* 4–5

Bog myrtle family Myricaceae

Trees and shrubs with aromatic leaves which have no stipules. The flowers have no sepals or petals and are in catkins.

Sweet gale

Myrica gale

♂

♀

Glands on twigs and lvs give sweet smell

Shrub. Male and female catkins on separate plants appear on tips of side shoots before the leaves, which are narrow, downy below and 2–5 cm long. *Ht:* 60–150 cm; *D:* N and W to S. Scand; *Fl:* 4–5

Hemp family Cannabaceae

Herbs with lobed leaves which have stipules. Male and female flowers are on separate plants. Stalked male and female flowers have parts in fives. The female flowers are unstalked.

Hop

Humulus lupulus

Fr cone-like, to 5 cm used in brewing

Lvs to 15 cm

♂ fls to 5 mm

Woody climber. The square stem is 3–6 m long and twists clockwise. Leaves placed opposite each other have 3–5 lobes and serrate edges. Stem and leaves are roughly hairy. *D:* T; *Fl:* 7–8

Nettle family Urticaceae

Herbs or shrubs, often with stinging hairs. Male and female flowers are in separate catkin-like structures. Flower parts are arranged in fours or fives; the male flowers have 4 or 5 stamens.

Stinging nettle	Annual nettle	Pellitory of the wall
Urtica dioica	*U. urens*	*Parietaria diffusa*

Perennial. Has creeping stems with erect shs at intervals. Stem and lvs have stinging hrs. All lvs have blades longer than stks. *Ht:* to 1.5 m; *D:* T; *Fl:* 6–8

Annual. Like *U. dioica* but less tall. Lower lvs have stks longer than blades. Each plant has both ♂ and ♀ fls on lfy branches. *Ht:* 45 cm; *D:* T; *Fl:* 6–9

Erect per covered in non-stinging hrs. ♂ fls borne on stem sides, ♀ fls on stem tips. *Ht:* to 1 m; *D:* T; *Fl:* 6–10

Mistletoe family Loranthaceae

Woody plants with undivided leaves. They are parasitic on trees but also have green tissues that can function normally. The fruit is a one-seeded berry.

Mistletoe

Viscum album

Woody evergreen to 1 m growing on tree branches, especially apple. Stklss ♂ and ♀ fls on separate plants. Leaves 2–8 cm long are opposite each other in pairs. Reputedly aphrodisiac. *D:* T (not N or E); *Fl:* 2–4

Birthwort family Aristolochiaceae

Herbs or woody climbers with leaves placed alternately on their stems. The flower-parts are three-lobed and arranged in a single whorl. The fruit is a capsule.

Asarabacca

Asarum europaeum

Low-growing per with thick creeping rhizome. Leaves kidney-shaped. Fls sol, brownish, hry on outside. *Ht:* to 5 cm; *D:* T to S Fennoscand; *Fl:* 5–8

Birthwort

Aristolochia clematitis

Perennial to 80 cm, distinctive smell. Has creeping rhizome and erect shs on which fls are borne. Fls to 3 cm, swollen at base. Lvs heart-shaped. *D:* C, S; *Fl:* 6–9

Dock family Polygonaceae

Herbs or shrubs with alternate leaves and sheathing stipules called ochreae. The flower parts, in threes or sixes, persist round the hard, often triangular fruit.

Common sorrel

Rumex acetosa

Sheep's sorrel

R. acetosella

Fiddle dock

R. pulcher

Erect, hrlss to 1 m. Lvs to 10 cm, downward-pointed lobes at base, upper lvs clasping; fr round. *D:* T; *Fl:* 5–6

Erect per to 30 cm. Lvs to 4 cm, basal lobes spreading. Top lvs do not clasp stem. *D:* T; *Fl:* 5–8

Flowers on spread brs that may tangle in fr. Fl parts toothed, fruit 3-warted. *Ht:* 40 cm; *D:* S, W; *Fl:* 7–8

Broad-leaved dock

R. obtusifolius

Erect per. Lvs broad, to 25 cm, hry below; fl parts toothed, fr 1-warted. *Ht:* 70 cm; *D:* T; *Fl:* 6–10

Golden dock

R. maritimus

Clustered dock

R. conglomeratus

Wood dock

R. sanguineus

Perennial to 50 cm in fr. Persistent, fine-toothed fl parts; fr 3-warted, long stkd. *D:* T (not far N); *Fl:* 6–9

Upright, brs spread; lf blade longer than stk; ptls untoothed, fr 3-warted. *Ht:* 55 cm; *D:* T (not far N); *Fl:* 7–8

Erect per to 1 m. Brs make acute angles with stem. Fl parts not toothed, 1 wart on fr. *D:* T; *Fl:* 6–8

15

Curled dock

Rumex crispus

Erect per. Lvs long, narrow, curled and crisp at the edges. Infl dense, little branched. Fruit has 3 warts and an edge without obvious teeth. *Ht:* 1 m; *D:* T; *Fl:* 7–9

Marsh dock

R. palustris

Upright ann or bi. 3-warted fr has short, thick stk. Fl parts around fr blunt-tipped with rigid teeth. Plant becomes yellow-brown in fruit. *Ht:* to 1 m; *D:* S; C; *Fl:* 6–9

Water dock

R. hydrolapathum

Robust per. Leaves to 1 m. Fruit 3-warted, 6–8 mm long, with triangular segments and a few short teeth. *Ht:* to 2 m; *D:* T (not far N); *Fl:* 7–9

Mountain sorrel

Oxyria digyna

Scottish dock

R. aquaticus

Robust per. Leaves triangular, tapering from base. Lf stks as long as blades. Frs untoothed, unwarted, borne on slender stalks. *Ht:* to 2 m; *D:* C, N, E; *Fl:* 7–8

Shore dock

R. rupestris

Erect per. Like *R. conglomeratus* (p 15) but brs almost vertical. Lvs blue-green. Fruit: 3-warted with untoothed margins. *Ht:* to 70 cm; *D:* W; *Fl:* 6–8

Hairless per. Lvs kidney-shaped. Fl and fr stks slender. Outer fl parts spread or bent back. Fruit is broad-winged. *Ht:* 25 cm; *D:* N, C, S; *Fl:* 7–8

Redshank

Polygonum persicaria

Hairless, branched per. Lvs lance-shaped, often with black blotch. Fl parts lack glands. Fr ridged. *Ht:* to 80 cm; *D:* T; *Fl:* 6–10

Bistort

P. bistorta

Hairless. Lvs narrow abruptly at base to winged stks. Infl dense, to 1.5 cm across. *Ht:* to 50 cm); *D:* C, N (not Scand); *Fl:* 6–8

Alpine bistort

P. viviparum

Creeping, some shoots upright. Lvs taper at base and tip. Fl head often has bulbils at base. *Ht:* to 40 cm; *D:* N, S; *Fl:* 6–8

Amphibious bistort

P. amphibium

Hairless, varies in form. On mud to 75 cm high, in water has floating lvs more tapered at their base. Fl has 5 protruding stamens. *D:* T; *Fl:* 7–9

Knotgrass

P. aviculare

Main stem lvs longer than branch leaves. Flowers single or in small clusters. *Ht:* to 1 m; *D:* T; *Fl:* 7–10

Pale persicaria

P. lapathifolium

Erect shs often hairy. Lvs to 20 cm may have central blotch. Yellow glands on pale fl parts. Infl dense. *Ht:* to 1 m; *D:* T; *Fl:* 6–10

Water pepper

P. hydropiper

Flowers in slim nodding head have yellow glands. Plant has a burning taste. *Ht:* to 75 cm; *D:* T (not N); *Fl:* 7–9

Buckwheat

Fagopyrum esculentum

Leaves broad, heart-shaped. Fr 2–3 times length of fl parts. Once widely cultivated. *Ht:* to 60 cm; *D:* T (not Fennoscand); *Fl:* 7–8

17

Goosefoot family Chenopodiaceae

Herbs or shrubs, often with fleshy stems and leaves. Plants look silvery or mealy. Leaves borne alternately have no stipules. The small, simple, greenish flowers have 3–5 lobes.

Nettle-leaved goosefoot

C. murale

Angular lvs with coarse, sharp teeth. Infl much branched. *Ht:* to 70 cm; *D:* T; *Fl:* 7–10

Red goosefoot

C. rubrum

Shining, reddish. Lvs angular with blunt teeth. Flower head dense. *Ht:* 50 cm; *D:* T; *Fl:* 7–9

Stinking goosefoot

C. vulvaria

Leaves toothless, mealy, with pointed tips. Plant smells of bad fish. *Ht:* 25 cm; *D:* T; *Fl:* 7–9

Many-seeded goosefoot

C. polyspermum

Leaves oval, toothless to 8 cm, not mealy. Stem 4-angled. *Ht:* to 1 m; *D:* T; *Fl:* 7–10

Fat hen

Chenopodium album

Variable ann. Stems erect, often red-tinged. Lvs dark green or mealy, angular, narrower in infl. Flower parts keeled. Ancient food plant replaced by spinach. *Ht:* to 1 m; *D:* T; *Fl:* 7–10

Common orache

Atriplex patula

Lf stks 1 cm long

Erect, branched, mealy ann. Upper lvs linear, lower have spreading basal lobes. Lfy structures present around fr. *Ht:* to 90 cm; *D:* T; *Fl:* 9–10

Grass-leaved orache

Atriplex littoralis

Annual. Linear, mealy lvs almost toothless. Rough lfy parts round fr. *Ht:* 70 cm; *D:* C, W, S; *Fl:* 7–8

Spear-leaved orache

A. hastata

Lower lvs triangular, mealy below; brs more uprt than *A. patula*. *Ht:* 80 cm; *D:* T; *Fl:* 8–9

Sea purslane

Halimione portulacoides

Lvs untoothed, mealy, elliptical

Perennial shrub. Infl dense at sh tips. Fr not stkd. *Ht:* to 1 m; *D:* N to Dk; *Fl:* 7–9

Annual seablite

Sueda maritima

Succulent, hrlss ann. Lvs to 4 cm, narrow, pointed. *Ht:* to 50 cm; *D:* T; *Fl:* 8–10

Glasswort

Salicornia europaea

Fls almost hidden at joints

Succulent ann. Stems and brs segmented, succ. Lvs tiny scales. Edible. *Ht:* 20 cm; *D:* T; *Fl:* 8–9

Prickly saltwort

Salsola kali

Prostrate ann. Leaves unstkd, with spine at tip. *Ht:* to 60 cm; *D:* T; *Fl:* 7–9

Sea beet

Beta maritima

Succulent, sprawling, often reddish. Basal lvs hrlss, not toothed, in a rosette. Infl dense, fls green. *Ht:* 1 m; *D:* N to S. Scand; *Fl:* 7–9

Purslane family Portulacaceae

Herbs, usually hairless, Flowers have 4–6 petals and two sepals distinguishing them from members of the pink family.

Blinks

Montia fontana

Fls *have 5 ptls, 3 smaller than the other 2*

Weak, straggling much–branched herb. Lvs opposite, egg-shaped. Fls in clusters. Spherical fr contains black seeds. *Ht:* to 50 cm; *D:* T; *Fl:* 5–10

Pink family Caryophyllaceae

Herbs with opposite leaves that have no lobes or teeth. Flowers with 4–5 unjoined petals and sepals are in clusters at shoot tips. Petals are often lobed at their tips.

Field mouse-ear

Cerastium arvense

Fr *cylindrical*

Sticky mouse-ear

C. glomeratum

Fr *ovoid*

Annual. Shs uprt. Stem lvs and spls hry. Ptls and spls equal in length. *Ht:* 25 cm; *D:* T (not NE); *Fl:* 4–9

Common mouse-ear

C. fontanum

Perennial herb. Brs prostrate to 30 cm. Unstkd, hry lvs to 2 cm. Fls in loose groups. Ptls 2 × length of spls. *D:* T (not far N); *Fl:* 4–8

Creeping hry per. Fl clusters spread out in fr. Ptls and spls equal length. *Ht:* 40 cm; *D:* T; *Fl:* 4–9

Alpine mouse-ear
C. alpinum

Sea mouse-ear
C. diffusum

Prostrate per. Dense
soft hrs on lvs. Ptls
2 × spls. *Ht:* 10 cm;
D: N, S; *Fl:* 6–8

Much branched ann. Lvs and shs dark green and
covered with hrs. Fls to 6 mm with 4 ptls shorter
than the 4 spls. *Ht:* 20 cm; *D:* S, W, C, N to
Swed; *Fl:* 5–7

Thyme-leaved sandwort
Arenaria serpyllifolia

Three-nerved sandwort
Moehringia trinervia

Leaves hry, pointed, to only 6 mm.
Fls 7 mm, ptls notched, shorter
than spls. *Ht:* 20 cm; *D:* T; *Fl:* 6–8

Weak ann. Lvs with 3 parallel veins.
Fl to 6 mm, ptls shorter than spls.
Ht: 25 cm; *D:* T; *Fl:* 5–6

Fringed sandwort
Arenaria ciliata

Mossy sandwort
Moehringia muscosa

Sea sandwort
Honkenya peploides

Prostrate hry per. Fls to
1 cm, 3 hry ridges on
spls. *Ht:* 6 cm; *D:* T
(local); *Fl:* 6–7

Prostrate hrlss per; 4
ptls 1.5 × length of
spls. Fr 4-toothed. *Ht:*
20 cm; *D:* C, S; *Fl:* 6–8

Prostrate, succ. Fls to
1 cm among lvs, ♂ and
♀ fls separate. *Ht:*
15 cm; *D:* NW; *Fl:* 5–8

Spring sandwort

Minuartia verna

Tufted per. Lvs and spls strongly 3-veined, lf tips pointed. Ptls just longer than spls. *Ht:* 10 cm; *D:* S, W, C; *Fl:* 5–9

Coral necklace

Illecebrum verticillatum

Creeping, hrlss. Lvs have oval stipules. Ptls longer than succ spls. *Ht:* 15 cm; *D:* W, C; *Fl:* 7–9

Lesser sea spurrey

Spergularia marina

Creeping brs to 20 cm. Lvs succ, pointed. Blunt ptls shorter than spls, less than 8 stms. *D:* T; *Fl:* 6–8

Mossy cyphel

M. sedoides

Densely tufted per. Makes cushions to 25 cm across by 8 cm high. Lvs succ. Fls to 5 mm diam with 5 spls, no ptls. *D:* Scotland, S, E; *Fl:* 6–8

Corn spurrey

Spergula arvensis

Stem has sticky hrs

Annual. Spreading brs from base. Lvs succ, grooved below. *Ht:* 25 cm; *D:* T; *Fl:* 6–8

Sea pearlwort

Sagina maritima

Leaves spineless. Fls on main stem only have 4 spls, no ptls. Many sim spp. *Ht:* 15 cm; *D:* N to S Fin; *Fl:* 5–9

Four-leaved allseed

Polycarpon tetraphyllum

Basal lvs *in whorl*

Hairless v branched; lvs oval, upper in opposite prs. Fls have 5 hooked spls. *Ht:* 10 cm; *D:* S, W; *Fl:* 6–7

Knotted pearlwort

S. nodosa

Delicate tufted per. Lvs spined, *c.* 1.5 cm at base, shorter above. Ptls 2 × spl length. *Ht:* 10 cm; *D:* T; *Fl:* 7–9

Smooth rupturewort

Herniaria glabra

Prostrate hrlss. Lvs opposite, to 1 cm long with stipules. Fls in dense clusters each 2 mm diam, 5 tiny ptls. *Ht:* 15 cm; *D:* T (not far N); *Fl:* 7

Marsh stitchwort

S. palustris

Creeping perennial. Untoothed lvs. Bracts have green stripe. Ptls v deeply cleft. *Ht:* 40 cm; *D:* N, C; *Fl:* 5–7

Greater stitchwort

S. holostea

Stems brittle, uprt, 4-angled. Lvs rough. Fls to 3 cm, ptls cut to half length, 10 stms, 3 styles. *Ht:* 45 cm; *D:* T (not far N); *Fl:* 4–6

Lesser stitchwort

S. graminea

Leaves toothless, hry at base. Colourless bracts. Fls to 1.2 cm, ptls and spls equal. *Ht:* 50 cm; *D:* T; *Fl:* 5–8

Upright chickweed

Moenchia erecta

Perennial. Erect stem to 12 cm. Lvs hairless, longest below. Fls to 8 mm, spls longer than ptls. *D:* W, C, N to Eng; *Fl:* 5–6

Common chickweed

Stellaria media

Weak ann. Stems have 1 line of hrs between lf pairs. Ptls cleft. Fr 6-lobed. *Ht:* to 40 cm; *D:* T; *Fl:* 1–12

Water chickweed

Myosoton aquaticum

Weak, spreading per. Shs to 1 m, hry above. Upper lvs unstkd; fls to 1.5 cm, lobed ptls 1.5 × spls. *D:* T (not far N); *Fl:* 7–8

23

White campion

Silene alba

Shoots erect, hry. Lvs hry to 10 cm, upper lvs unstkd. Fl to 3 cm, spls a tube. Separate ♂ and ♀ plants. *Ht:* 60 cm; *D:* T; *Fl:* 5–9

Bladder campion

S. vulgaris

Branched per. Upper lvs unstkd, blue-green. Infl much branched with inflated spl tube and colourless bracts. Fl to 1.8 cm. *Ht:* 60 cm; *D:* T; *Fl:* 6–8

Red campion

S. dioica

Like *S. alba.* Stems hry. Winged stks on basal lvs. Teeth on fr curled back. *Ht:* 60 cm; *D:* T; *Fl:* 5–6

White sticky catchfly

S. viscosa

Basal lvs have wavy edges

Plant covered in dense, sticky hrs. Infl looks whorled. Ptls lobed. *Ht:* to 60 cm; *D:* C, E; *Fl:* 6–7

Northern catchfly

S. wahlbergella

Unbranched per, less than 30 cm. Ptls just outside swollen spl tube. *D:* Arct; *Fl:* 6–8

Sand catchfly

S. conica

Very sticky, hry ann. Fl to 5 mm, spl tube hry, conical. *Ht:* 25 cm; *D:* C, S; *Fl:* 5–6

Forked catchfly

S. dichotoma

Stems hry. Branched infl, 5–10 fls per br. Spl tube hry. *Ht:* 60 cm; *D:* E; *Fl:* 5–8

Spanish catchfly

S. otites

Sticky hrs on stem. Basal lvs spathulate. Many 4 mm fls in infl, spl tube hrlss. ♂ and ♀ separate. *Ht:* 55 cm; *D:* C, S, E; *Fl:* 6–9

Moss campion

S. acaulis

Cushion-forming. Lvs v narrow in rosettes. Fls single to 1.2 cm. Spl tube often reddish, wider at mouth. *Ht:* 8 cm; *D:* Arct, C, W; *Fl:* 7–8

Nottingham catchfly

S. nutans

Perennial. Erect shoots have sticky hrs above. Lvs hry, basal lvs long-stkd. Ptls narrow, v cut, lobes inrolled. *Ht:* 60 cm; *D:* T; *Fl:* 5–7

Sea campion

S. maritima

Cushion-forming. Lvs stiff. Fls 2.5 cm, 4 per infl. Bracts lf-like. Fr 6-toothed. *Ht:* 15 cm; *D:* W; *Fl:* 6–8

Rock catchfly

S. rupestris

Short per. Lvs narrow. Infl spread, fls long-stkd, ptls notched but not deeply lobed. *Ht:* 15 cm; *D:* Fennoscand, W, C; *Fl:* 6–9

Creeping gypsophila

Gypsophila repens

Creeping hrlss per. Up to 30 fls in infl, fl stks 2 × length of spl tube, 2 styles. *Ht:* 20 cm; *D:* C; *Fl:* 6–9

Annual gypsophila

G. muralis

Very branched ann, hrlss above. Infl loose, fls to 4 mm, ptls 2 × spl length. *Ht:* 20 cm; *D:* C, E; *Fl:* 6–10

Tunic flower

Petrorhagia saxifraga

Ptls to 1 cm

Hairless ann, narrow lvs. Spl tube 5-toothed, 5-veined. Spls half ptl length. *Ht:* to 45 cm; *D:* C, S; *Fl:* 6–8

Cheddar pink

D. gratianopolitanus

Fl to 2.5 cm

Tussocky. Prostrate non-flowering shs. Fl shs uprt, hrlss. Fls sol, 4–6 scales. *Ht:* 15 cm; *D:* W, C; *Fl:* 6–7

Maiden pink

D. deltoides

Tufted, roughly hry. Fls have 2–4 scales half spl length. *Ht:* 30 cm; *D:* T; *Fl:* 6–9

Soapwort

Saponaria officinalis

Hairless lvs to 10 cm. Infl dense, no scales below spls. *Ht:* 60 cm; *D:* T (not N); *Fl:* 7–9

Large pink

Dianthus superbus

Fl to 6 cm

Branched. Lvs linear. Ptls very cut, 2–4 scales round spls. *Ht:* 70 cm; *D:* C, N; *Fl:* 6–9

Carthusian pink

D. carthusianorum

Erect, hrlss per. Lvs long, pointed. Fls well clustered. Scales half spl length. *Ht:* 40 cm; *D:* S, W, C; *Fl:* 5–8

Corn cockle

Agrostemma githago

Unbranched stem and fl stks have white hrs. Spls long, pointed. *Ht:* to 1 m; *D:* S; *Fl:* 6–8

Deptford pink

D. armeria

Fl to 1.3 cm

Leaves on stem linear, hry. Fls grouped; 2 hry scales as long as spl tube. *Ht:* 45 cm; *D:* T (rare in N); *Fl:* 7–8

Jersey pink

D. gallicus

Tufted, lvs blunt. Ptl tips shredded; 4 small scales; fragrant. *Ht:* 35 cm; *D:* W; *Fl:* 6–8

Ragged Robin

Lychnis flos-cuculi

Tall, branched per. Lvs rough, basal lvs stkd. Spls in ribbed tube. *Ht:* 60 cm; *D:* T; *Fl:* 5–6

Alpine catchfly

L. alpina

Leaves in basal rosette. Dense infl of *c.* 20 fls, ptls 2-lobed. *Ht:* 10 cm; *D:* N, S; *Fl:* 6–7

Sticky catchfly	**Flower of Jove** 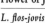
L. viscaria	*L. flos-jovis*

Sticky hrs on upper stem. Infl of 3–6 short-stkd fls; ptls notched, spl tube long. *Ht:* 60 cm; *D:* T; *Fl:* 5–6

Branched per. Long-stkd fls in flat-topped infl. Ptls to 1 cm, deeply 2-lobed. *Ht:* 60 cm; *D:* C; *Fl:* 6–8

Water lily family Nymphaceae

Perennial aquatics with submerged rhizomes and floating leaves. Single flowers have 3–6 sepals and three or more petals.

White water lily

Nymphaea alba

Circular floating lvs to 30 cm across deeply cleft at attachment to lf stk. Fls to 20 cm across have 4 spls and many ptls. *D:* T; *Fl:* 7–8

Yellow water lily

Nuphar lutea

Floating lvs oval, to 40 cm across, cleft at base. Fls to 6 cm, raised above water, have 5–6 spls and many ptls a third of spl length. *D:* T; *Fl:* 7–8

Hornwort family Ceratophyllaceae

Submerged perennial aquatics with whorled leaves split into narrow lobes. Solitary, inconspicuous male and female flowers are borne in the leaf nodes on separate plants.

Rigid hornwort

Ceratophyllum demersum

Lvs to 2 cm

Stiff waterweed, some stems to 1 m long. Lvs serrate, divided once or twice. Fr oval, to 4 mm, 2 spines at base but hard to see. *D:* T; *Fl:* 7–9

Buttercup family Ranunculaceae

Herbs, woody plants and climbers often poisonous and usually with spirally arranged leaves without stipules. The flowers vary widely but have many stamens and tend to attract insects.

Meadow buttercup

Ranunculus acris

Lvs on stem deeply cut

Erect per. Stem branched, hry. Basal lvs not cut. Fls to 2.5 cm on hry, unridged stks. Spls hry, uprt. *Ht:* to 1 m; *D:* T; *Fl:* 6–7

Large white buttercup

R. platanifolius

Tall per to 1.3 m, hry below. Lvs have 5–7 palmate lobes not deeply cut. Fls to 2 cm, ptls small, fl stks 4–5 × lf length. *D:* C, S; *Fl:* 5–8

Goldilocks buttercup

R. auricomus

Hairy per. Upper lvs 3-lobed. Up to 5 ptls of uneven size. *Ht:* 30 cm; *D:* T; *Fl:* 4–5

Celery-leaved buttercup

R. sceleratus

Robust ann. Stems hollow, furrowed. Ptls small. To 100 or more frs per head. *Ht:* 45 cm; *D:* T; *Fl:* 7–9

Corn buttercup

R. arvensis

Branched. Upper lvs 3-lobed. Fl stks hry, fr spined. *Ht:* 80 cm; *D:* S, W, C; *Fl:* 6–7

Bulbous buttercup

R. bulbosus

Bulbous swelling at sh base. Spls bent back, hry below. *Ht:* 35 cm; *D:* T; *Fl:* 5–6

Glacial buttercup

R. glacialis

Perennial. Lvs and stem hrlss. Lvs fleshy, 3-lobed. Fls sol, spls hry, uprt. *Ht:* 15 cm; *D:* N, C; *Fl:* 6–8

Lesser celandine

R. ficaria

Has many rt tubers and may be bulbils in axils. Fls sol, 8–12 ptls. *Ht:* 20 cm; *D:* T; *Fl:* 3–5

Lesser spearwort

R. flammula

Lower stems have rts. Upper stems hollow, hrlss above. Basal lvs spear-shaped. *Ht:* 50 cm; *D:* T; *Fl:* 6–8

Greater spearwort

R. lingua

Creeping buttercup

R. repens

Erect per to 60 cm. Creeping runners root at nodes. Basal lvs 3-lobed, middle lobe stkd. Fl stks ridged, hry. Spls uprt or spread. *D:* T; *Fl:* 5–8

Branched per. Uprt, near-hrlss, hollow stems to 1.2 m rise from creeping base. Stem lvs unstkd. Fl 4 cm. *D:* T; *Fl:* 6–9

Water crowfoot

Ranunculus aquatilis

Floating lvs
lobed

Branched, hrlss. Fine-cut under-
water lvs in many planes. Fls 3 cm,
15 + long stamens. *D:* T; *Fl:* 5–8

Ivy-leaved crowfoot

R. hederaceus

Fl to 6 mm,
6–10 stms

Branched per. Creeping stems to
40 cm. Lvs opp, stkd, 3–5 lobed.
No submerged lvs. *D:* T; *Fl:* 6–9

River water crowfoot

R. fluitans

Fls to 3 cm, many
short stms

Robust waterweed with deeply divided submerged lvs to 30 cm with a few
long segments. Stems to 6 m. Usually no floating lvs. *D:* W, C; *Fl:* 6–8

Wood anemone

Anemone nemorosa

Fls have
6–7 pts,
no spls

Perennial. Lvs borne on creeping
rhizome and fl stems. Fls to 4 cm,
sol. *Ht:* 20 cm; *D:* T; *Fl:* 3–5

Yellow anemone

A. ranunculoides

Stem lvs on v short stks. One or
more fls per fl stk. Fls 2 cm diam, 5
ptls. *Ht:* 20 cm; *D:* T; *Fl:* 3–5

Blue anemone

A. apennina

Dark rhizome. Lvs
hry below. Fls sol,
10–15 ptls. *Ht:* 20 cm;
D: S; *Fl:* 3–4

Narcissus-flowered anemone

A. narcissiflora

Robust, hry. Basal lvs stkd, stem lvs unstkd. Fls
to 3 cm on 4 cm stks. *Ht:* 30 cm; *D:* T; *Fl:* 6–7

Palmate anemone

A. palmata

Stem hry. Basal leaves shallow-lobed. Fls 3 cm, 10–15 ptls. *Ht:* 20 cm; *D:* SW; *Fl:* 2–6

Snowdrop windflower

A. sylvestris

Fl to 7 cm,

Hairy, has rt buds. Basal lvs long-stalked, lobed; fl sol. *Ht:* 35 cm; *D:* C, E; *Fl:* 2–6

Marsh marigold

Caltha palustris

Hairless. Lvs round or kidney-shaped, fine teeth; no true ptls. *Ht:* 20 cm; *D:* T; *Fl:* 3–7

Forking larkspur

Consolida regalis

Fl *long-spurred*

Annual. Brs spread, hry. Few fls in infl, fr single, hrlss. *Ht:* 40 cm; *D:* S, W, C, E; *Fl:* 6–7

Eastern larkspur

C. orientalis

Sticky hrs on shoots. Many fls in infl. Spur short. Fr hry, beaked. *Ht:* 70 cm; *D:* S; *Fl:* 6–7

Alpine larkspur

Delphinium elatum

Stem hrlss above. Upper lvs short-stkd; 3 hrlss frs per fl. *Ht:* to 2 m; *D:* C, S; *Fl:* 6–8

Columbine

Aquilega vulgaris

Leaves long-stkd, hrlss, lflts stkd. Spurs knobbed. *Ht:* 70 cm; *D:* W, C; *Fl:* 5–6

Monkshood

Aconitum napellus

Leaves deeply lobed. Wide hoods on fls; 3 frs per fl. *Ht:* 70 cm; *D:* W C; *Fl:* 5–6

Love-in-a-mist

Nigella damascena

Finely cut lvs, some under fls. Ptls clawed. Fr 5-membered. *Ht:* 20 cm; *D:* S; *Fl:* 6–7

Globe flower

Trollius europaeus

Erect hrlss per. Basal lvs stkd, stem lvs unstkd. Fls consist of spls and nectaries. *Ht:* 40 cm; *D:* T (not far N); *Fl:* 6–8

Pasque flower

Pulsatilla vulgaris

Has rosette of long-stkd, hry, v cut lvs. Fls sol, 8 cm; ptls hry to 3 × stamen length. *Ht:* 20 cm; *D:* NW; *Fl:* 4–5

Pale pasque flower

P. vernalis

Perennial to 15 cm but to 35 cm in fr. Basal lvs evergreen. Fls to 6 cm nodding at first, then erect. *D:* C, N; *Fl:* 4–6

Small pasque flower

P. pratensis

Small per to 10 cm but to 45 cm in fr. Lvs hry, v cut. Fls to 4 cm, ptls under 1.5 times stamen length. *D:* C, E; *Fl:* 5

Alpine pasque flower

P. alpina

Stems to 45 cm with long-stkd, hry doubly cut basal lvs. Stem lvs stkd unlike other spp. Fls to 6 cm, erect. *D:* C, S; *Fl:* 5–7

Winter aconite

Eranthis hyemalis

Hairless per. Lvs palmately 3–5 lobed, arise after fls. Spls 6, ptl-like, 30 stamens, 6 carpels, fls to 3 cm. *Ht:* 10 cm; *D:* C, S, W; *Fl:* 1–3

Stinking hellebore

Helleborus foetidus

Strong-smelling per to 80 cm. Basal lvs evergreen, topmost lvs small, undivided. Fls 3 cm, many per sh, never wide open. *D:* S, W; *Fl:* 3–4

Christmas rose

H. niger

Perennial. Basal lvs evergreen, stem lvs rounded, not divided. Fls to 10 cm, 2–3 per shoot, usually 7 carpels. *Ht:* 20 cm; *D:* E, S; *Fl:* 1–4

Summer pheasant's eye

Adonis aestivalis

Erect ann. Lvs v cut. Fls 2 cm, 5 spls cling to spread ptls. *Ht:* 25 cm; *D:* T (not N); *Fl:* 6–8

Green hellebore

H. viridis

Erect per to 40 cm. Lvs long-stkd, hrlss, serrate, palmately divided. Fls to 5 cm, wide-spread ptls and 3 carpels. *D:* W, C; *Fl:* 3–4

Pheasant's eye

A. annua

Upright ann. Lvs hrlss, v cut. Fls to 2 cm, spls do not touch ptls. *Ht:* 25 cm; *D:* S; *Fl:* 6–8

Yellow pheasant's eye

A. vernalis

Erect per to 40 cm, base scaly. Stem lvs unstkd, cut twice. Ptls 2 × spl length. *D:* E, S, C; *Fl:* 4–5

Peony

Paeonia officinalis

Woody stemmed perennial. Lower lvs hrlss above, cut into 17–30 segments. Fl to 1.3 cm, fr has 2–3 hry follicles. *Ht:* 50 cm; *D:* S; *Fl:* 5–6

Hepatica

Hepatica nobilis

Lvs and fls arise direct from short stock. Lvs 3-lobed, purplish below. Fl 2 cm, 3 bracts. *Ht:* 10 cm; *D:* T (not far N); *Fl:* 3–5

Common meadow rue

T. flavum

Baneberry

Actaea spicata

Strong smelling. Lvs pinnate. Infl dense, long stamens, fruit a berry. *Ht:* 40 cm; *D:* T; *Fl:* 5–6

Lesser meadow rue

Thalictrum minus

Tufted perennial. Lvs pinnate, 3–4 × divided, lflts as broad as long. Infl loose, drooping stamens, fr uprt. *Ht:* 85 cm; *D:* T; *Fl:* 6–8

Leaves cut 2–3 × , lower stkd; lflts longer than broad. Infl dense, stms erect. *Ht:* 75 cm; *D:* T; *Fl:* 7–8

Alpine meadow rue

T. alpinum

Slender per to 15 cm. Lvs 2 × cut mostly arise from a rhizome. Stamens hanging, yellow and purple stks. *D:* N, C; *Fl:* 6–7

Mousetail

Myosurus minimus

Hairless ann. Narrow undivided lvs in basal rosette. Fls small, in a spike, 5–10 stamens. *Ht:* 9 cm; *D:* T; *Fl:* 6–7

Traveller's joy

Clematis vitalba

Woody climbing per, stems to 30 m. Lvs have 5 coarsely toothed lflts. Fls to 2 cm, 4 hry ptls, long feathery styles on fr. *D:* T (not N); *Fl:* 7–8

Poppy family Papaveraceae

Herbs with deeply divided leaves. True poppies have a milky juice in all parts but the fumitories (now part of the family) do not. Flowers have 4 petals and two or many stamens.

Common poppy

Papaver rhoeas

Fr a rounded capsule

Fl 7–10 cm diam

Erect, branching annual to 60 cm. Stems covered in spreading, bristly hrs. Lvs compound, pinnately divided, large central lobe. *D:* T; *Fl:* 6–8

Arctic poppy	Long-headed poppy	Prickly poppy
P. radicatum	*P. dubium*	*P. argemone*

Tufted per, juice yellow. Lf bases persist as a sheath. Fl to 5 cm, fr a bristly elliptic-ovoid capsule. *Ht:* 15 cm; *D:* NW; *Fl:* 7

Erect branched ann, flat hrs above. Fr to 2.5 cm, 2× as long as wide. *Ht:* 40 cm; *D:* T; *Fl:* 6–7

Upright ann to 45 cm, flat tips v pointed. Lf tips v pointed. Fl to 6 cm; fr ridged, bristly to 2.5 cm. *D:* S; *Fl:* 6–7

Welsh poppy   Yellow horned poppy   Red horned poppy

Meconopsis cambrica   *Glaucium flavum*   *G. corniculatum*

Tufted, hrlss stems to 60 cm. Basal lvs long-stkd. Fls to 8 cm, 2 hry spls, 4 ptls; fr oval, 4–6 valves. *D:* W; *Fl:* 6–8

Branched, glaucous, to 90 cm, basal lvs hry. Fls short-stkd, fr to 30 cm. *D:* W; *Fl:* 6–9

Branched ann to 30 cm. Bristly spreading hrs on stems and lvs. Fls to 5 cm, short-stkd; fr to 22 cm. *D:* S; *Fl:* 6–7

Greater celandine

Chelidonium majus

Stems fragile to 90 cm, scattered hrs. Orange sap. Fls to 2 cm, fr to 5 cm. *D:* T; *Fl:* 5–8

Bulbous corydalis

Corydalis solida

Erect to 20 cm. Lobed bracts below fls. *D:* T (not far N); *Fl:* 4–5. *C. bulbosa* sim but bracts unlobed

Climbing corydalis

C. claviculata

Yellow corydalis

C. lutea

 Infl of 6–10 fls

Common fumitory

Fumaria officinalis

Scrambling, lvs end in tendril. Ptl tube short-spurred, 6 fls in infl. *Ht:* 50 cm; *D:* W; *Fl:* 6–9

Branched, no tendrils. Ptl tube short-spurred to 1.8 cm. *Ht:* to 30 cm; *D:* W, C; *Fl:* 5–8

Scrambling, hrlss. Lvs cut 2 × into linear lobes. Ptl tube 8 mm, 2 spls 10–40 fls per infl. Fr a nutlet. *Ht:* 10 cm; *D:* T; *Fl:* 5–10

Cabbage family Cruciferae

Annuals and perennials with spirally arranged leaves. The flowers have 4 sepals, 4 unjoined petals, 6 stamens and one stigma. The fruit opens by two valves. Many are weeds.

Wallflower

Cheiranthus cheiri

Erect branched perennial to 60 cm. Stems woody and ridged. Basal lvs 5–10 cm long, undivided and covered with forked hairs. Flowers to 2.5 cm diam, ptls twice sepal length. Fruit 3–7 cm long. *D:* W, S, C; *Fl:* 4–6

Shepherd's purse

Capsella bursa-pastoris

Stem lvs clasping with pointed lobes. Ptls 2× spl length, fr 9 mm. *Ht:* 25 cm; *D:* T; *Fl:* 1–12

Hairy rocket

Erucastrum gallicum

Fr to 4 cm, curved

Erect ann to 60 cm, hrs point down. Lobed lvs, bracts at infl base. Fls 8 mm, slender beak on fr. *D:* SW, C; *Fl:* 5–9

Annual wall rocket

Diplotaxis muralis

Fl 1 cm

Fr 3–4 cm

Stems to 60 cm, bristly below. Toothed lvs to 10 cm. Strong-smelling. Ptls 2× spl length. *D:* S, C; *Fl:* 6–9

Small alison

Alyssum alyssoides

Fr to 4 mm

Lvs less than 2 cm

Erect ann, star-shaped hrs on shs. Fls 3 mm, spls persist in fr. *Ht:* 15 cm; *D:* T; *Fl:* 5–6

London rocket

Sisymbrium irio

 Fr to 5 cm

Lower lvs stkd, lobed, stem lvs stkd. No bracts. Fls 4 mm. *Ht:* 40 cm; *D:* T (not far N); *Fl:* 6–8

Hedge mustard

Sisymbrium officinale

Fl 3 mm

Stiffly erect ann to 90 cm. Downward-pointing hrs on stems, basal lvs in rosette, deeply lobed, no bracts. Fr narrow, erect. *D:* T; *Fl:* 6–8

Field pepperwort

Lepidium campestre

Upper lvs clasp stem

Has short, spreading hrs. Lvs unlobed. Fr notched at tip, spotted white. *Ht:* 40 cm; *D:* T; *Fl:* 5–8

Sea kale

Crambe maritima

Fr to 1.4 cm

Basal lvs to 30 cm

Erect per to 60 cm. Basal lvs long-stkd, glaucous. Ptls have green claws, fr 1-seeded. *D:* T; *Fl:* 6–8

Sea rocket

Cakile maritima

Fr to 2.5 cm does not split

Lvs lobed or toothed

Often prostrate succ to 45 cm. Infl dense, fr in 2 sections, 1 seed in each. *D:* T (not far N); *Fl:* 6–8

Dittander

L. latifolium

Branched, hrlss. Basal lvs serrate. Spls white-edged, fr unnotched. *Ht:* 1 m; *D:* T (not N); *Fl:* 6–7

Flixweed

Descurainia sophia

Lvs v divided

Erect with star-shaped hrs. Fls 3 mm, fr 2 cm, strong midrib. *Ht:* 60 cm; *D:* T; *Fl:* 6–8

Sea stock

Matthiola sinuata

Stem lvs elliptical

Branched hrs on stems, sticky hrs on stem lvs. Basal lvs wavy. Fls *c.* 2.5 cm, fr 10 cm. *Ht:* 40 cm; *D:* W, S; *Fl:* 6–8

Hoary whitlow grass

Draba incana

Fr to 9 mm, twisted, elliptic

Basal lvs serrate with star-shaped hrs. Fls 5 mm, ptls just notched. *Ht:* 30 cm; *D:* N, mts in C, W; *Fl:* 6–8

Yellow whitlow grass

D. aizoides

Fl stems lflss

Fl to 9 mm

Hairless per. Tufted rosette of stiff, linear lvs, keeled, white spine at tip. Fr 1 cm. *Ht:* 7 cm; *D:* C, S; *Fl:* 3–5

Alpine whitlow grass

D. alpina

Fr hrlss

Lvs in dense rosettes

Ptls to 5 mm

Represents complex group of spp. All have star-shaped hrs on leaves. *Ht:* 15 cm; *D:* Arct; *Fl:* 7–8

Common whitlow grass

Erophila verna

Fr long-stkd

Fl 4 mm

Variable low, hry ann. Lvs in basal rosette. Ptls v deeply cut, fr elliptic, hrlss. *Ht:* to 20 cm; *D:* T; *Fl:* 3–5

Common scurvy grass

Cochlearia officinalis

Basal lvs long-stkd. Upper lvs clasping. Fr 5 mm. *Ht:* 35 cm; *D:* NW; *Fl:* 5–8

English scurvy grass

C. anglica

Basal lvs taper to stk. Fls to 1.4 cm, fr oval, flattened, 1 cm. *Ht:* 25 cm; *D:* NW; *Fl:* 4–7

Alpine scurvy grass

C. pyrenaica

Very like *C. officinalis* and possibly the same sp as *C. alpina*. Lvs not succ. Fr tapers into stk and tip. *Ht:* 25 cm; *D:* C, W; *Fl:* 5–8

Arabis turrita

Lvs have
star-shaped hrs

Fr compressed,
no beak

Fl 1 cm

Biennial or per, horizontal at base with veg rosettes. Hry erect fl shs to 70 cm. Basal lvs serrate, narrow to stk, stem lvs oblong. *D:* C, S; *Fl:* 5–8

Hairy rock cress

A. hirsuta

Stems to 60 cm from rosette of obovate stkd lvs, hrs star-shaped; fr 4 cm. *D:* T; *Fl:* 6–8

Alpine rock cress

A. alpina

Creeping, erect fl shs to 40 cm. Basal lvs serrate, stkd. Fr 4 cm, spreading. *D:* N, W, S; *Fl:* 6–8

Great yellowcress

Rorippa amphibia

Hollow hrlss stems to 1.2 m. Ptls 2 × length of spls, fr long-stkd. *D:* T (not far N); *Fl:* 6–8

Marsh yellowcress

R. islandica

Ridged stems to 60 cm. Lower lvs stkd, v cut. Ptls equal spls in length, fr curved. *D:* T; *Fl:* 6–9

Thale cress

Arabidopsis thaliana

Erect shs to 50 cm, hry below; stem lvs unstkd. Fr 1.5 cm, erect on spread stks. *D:* (not far N); *Fl:* 4–5 (and 9–10)

Swine cress

Coronopus squamatus

Fr 3 mm

Prostrate lfy shs 20 cm. Lvs pinnately lobed. Infl unstkd, mostly opp lvs; fr short-stkd. *D:* W, C, S; *Fl:* 6–9

Watercress

Nasturtium officinale

Lvs pinnate

Hollow hrlss shs creep and float. Fr has 2 rows of seeds. *Ht:* 40 cm; *D:* T (not N); *Fl:* 5–10

Coralroot bittercress

C. bulbifera

Has bulbils in stem lf axils. Shs to 70 cm. Ptls 1.5 cm, 3 × spl length. *D:*T (not far N); *Fl:* 4–6

Hairy bittercress

C. hirsuta

Stems hrlss. Fls have 4 stamens; fr grows above fls. *Ht:* 20 cm; *D:* T (not far N); *Fl:* 4–7

Common wintercress

Barbarea vulgaris

Erect, hrlss, branched to 90 cm. Basal lvs stkd in rosette. Fr erect, 4-angled. *D:* T; *Fl:* 5–8

Large bittercress

C. amara
Lower lvs stkd pinnate

Creeping; erect shs to 60 cm. Fr 3 cm, long persistent style. *D:* T (not far N); *Fl:* 4–6

Cuckoo flower

Cardamine pratense

Erect per to 60 cm. Top lflt kidney-shaped. Fls long-stkd, ptls 3 × spl length, valves of fr curl up. *D:* T; *Fl:* 4–6

Wavy bittercress

C. flexuosa

Lvs pinnate, basal lvs stkd

Stems to 50 cm may be hry; ptls same length as spls, 6 stamens. Fr hardly extends above fls. *D:* W; *Fl:* 4–9

Field pennycress

Thlaspi arvense

Fr to 2.2 cm, tip notched

Erect, stems to 60 cm. Basal lvs broad, taper to stk. Fl 5 mm, fr broad-winged. *D:* T; *Fl:* 5–7

Hoary cress

Cardaria draba

Creeping. Uprt lfy shs to 90 cm. Basal lvs stkd, upper lvs clasping. Fr does not split. *D:* T; *Fl:* 5–6

Horse radish

Armoracia rusticana

Wild radish

Raphanus raphanistrum

Bristly, basal lvs have large top lobe. Ptls veined. Long-beaked fr splits crosswise. *Ht:* 40 cm; *D:* T; *Fl:* 5–9

Robust hrlss. Rts fleshy, edible. Basal lvs 40 cm, wavy-edged. Infl v branched. *Ht:* 1 m; *D:* T; *Fl:* 5–6

Sea radish

R. maritimus

Bristly hrs above. Ptls *c.* 2 cm, not veined. Fr short-beaked, does not split. *D:* W, N to GB; *Fl:* 6–8

Charlock

Sinapis arvensis

Fr 3 cm, veined, bristly

Stems to 80 cm with bristly hrs. Basal lvs lobed, upper lvs serrate, unlobed. Fr smooth. *D:* T; *Fl:* 5–7

White mustard

Sinapis alba

Like *S. arvensis* (p 42) but all lvs pinnately lobed. Fr beaked. *Ht:* 60 cm; *D:* T; *Fl:* 6–8

Wild cabbage

Brassica oleracea

Fr 5–10 cm, short break

Thick rootstock, stem has lf scars. Lower lvs large, few basal lobes, upper lvs stkd, oblong. Ptls 2 cm. *Ht:* to 3 m; *D:* W, N to GB; *Fl:* 5–8

Black mustard

Brassica nigra

Annual to 1 m, bristly below. No thick rootstock, all lvs stkd. Ridged fr held near stem. *D:* T; *Fl:* 6–9

Buckler mustard

Biscutella laevigata

Fr to 1.4 cm diam

Basal rosette of unlobed, possibly wavy lvs. Fr of 2 fused discs. *Ht:* 30 cm; *D:* C, S; *Fl:* 5–8

Garlic mustard

Alliaria petiolata

Roots and lvs smell of garlic. Stem hry. Fr 4-angled. *Ht:* 1 m; *D:* T (not far N); *Fl:* 4–6

Ball mustard

Neslia paniculata

Annual to 80 cm with star-shaped hrs. Fr wrinkled, does not split. *D:* C, E; *Fl:* 6–9

Treacle mustard

Erysimum cheiranthoides

Leafy stem to 90 cm, hrs branched. Basal lvs die when infl formed; fr 4-angled. *D:* T; *Fl:* 6–8

Perennial honesty

Lunaria rediviva

Woad

Isatis tinctoria

Fr
to 2 cm

Plant
used
as dye

Erect to 1.4 m. Top lvs stkd (unlike
L. annua). Infl at apex, fr oval. *D:* T
(not far N); *Fl:* 4–6

Hairless, several basal rosettes, stem
lvs arrow-shaped, hanging fr. *Ht:*
1 m; *D:* T (not N); *Fl:* 7–8

Mignonette family Resedaceae

Herbs with simple or divided spirally arranged leaves. Flowers
have 4–7 unfused petals and sepals, many stamens and 3–6 carpels
fusing into a one-celled capsule.

Wild mignonette

Reseda lutea

Fr to 1.8 cm,
3 lobes at tip

Upright mignonette

R. alba

Branched, erect, hrlss to 75 cm.
Basal lvs in rosette, pinnate stem lvs.
Fl 6 mm, 6 ptls and spls, fr erect. *D:*
S, W, C; *Fl:* 6–8

Leaves deeply cut into narrow
pinnate lobes. Fls 9 mm, 5 ptls, fr
oblong, 4 lobes at tip. *Ht:* 75 cm; *D:*
S, C, NW; *Fl:* 6–8

Rampion mignonette

Reseda phyteuma

Fr to 1.4 cm

Branched to 30 cm. Lvs unlobed or in prs, blunt lobes above; 6 ptls, fr drooping, 3-lobed. *D:* S; *Fl:* 6–8

Weld

R. luteola

Fr erect, 3 lobes above

Lvs narrow, wavy margins

Erect, hrlss to 1.5 m, little or not branched. Lf rosette in 1st yr, fl sh in 2nd. *D:* S, W, C; *Fl:* 6–8

Sundew family Droseraceae

Perennial herbs. The leaves have sticky hairs for trapping insects and are curled in bud. Flowers have 4–8 petals.

Common sundew

Drosera rotundifolia

Fl 5 mm diam

Perennial with low rosettes of leaves each 1 cm across with a long hry stk and circular blade. Erect fl shs to 25 cm and more than 2 × lf length from rosette centre. Fr pointed. *D:* T; *Fl:* 6–8

Great sundew

D. anglica   **Lf** blades to 3 cm

Erect lvs narrow to hrlss stks. Fl sh 2 × lf length from rosette centre; fr round. *D:* N, C; *Fl:* 7–8

Oblong-leaved sundew

D. intermedia

Lf stk hrlss

Oblong lvs *c.* 10 cm just shorter than fl sh arising under rosette, fr pointed *D:* N, W, C; *Fl:* 7–8

Stonecrop family Crassulaceae

Usually succulent herbs with undivided leaves. The flowers generally have 5 sepals and petals but may be more. The stamens are equal to or double the petals in number and there are as many unjoined carpels as petals.

Biting stonecrop

Sedum acre

Fl *1.2 cm*

Creeping evergreen to 10 cm. Shs erect, hrlss; lvs unstkd; 5 ptls and pointed spls. *D:* T; *Fl:* 6–7

Alpine stonecrop

S. alpestre

Spls *blunt*

Hairless; non-flowering shs v short, fl shs to 8 cm. Lvs unstkd, slightly flat. *D:* C, S; *Fl:* 6–7

English stonecrop

S. anglicum

Patch-forming, hrlss. Lvs globular, alternate. Fl stks short. *Ht:* 4 cm; *D:* W, N to Swed; *Fl:* 6–9

White stonecrop

S. album

Lvs *1 cm, unstkd*

Carpet-forming evergreen to 15 cm. Infl much branched, flat-topped, fl 9 mm. *D:* T (not NE); *Fl:* 6–8

Rose-root

Rhodiola rosea

Lvs *to 4 cm, toothed*

Fls *have 4 ptls and spls*

Robust, erect, glaucous per; short stock bears lf scars. Lvs flat, round. ♂ and ♀ separate. *Ht:* 22 cm; *D:* N, mts in C; *Fl:* 5–8

Rock stonecrop

S. forsteranum

Lvs to 2 cm, fine points

Fl 1.2 cm, 6–8 ptls

Creeping, glaucous. Old lvs stay on stems, new ones arise at tips. *Ht:* 22 cm; *D:* W; *Fl:* 6–7

Navelwort

Umbilicus rupestris

Hairless, usually unbranched. Lf blade circular, central stk; fl tubular. *Ht:* 30 cm; *D:* S, W; *Fl:* 6–8

Mossy stonecrop

Crassula tillaea

Dwarf, hrlss. Shs creeping, often reddish. Lvs and fls dense, 3 ptls and spls. *Ht:* 4 cm; *D:* S, W; *Fl:* 6–7

Reflexed stonecrop

S. reflexum

Fl 1.4 cm, 7 ptls and spls

Lvs not flat

More robust than *S. forsteranum*. Top lvs bent back at tip, dead lvs fall off. *Ht:* 25 cm; *D:* C; *Fl:* 6–8. *S. telephium* (orpine) sim but pinks fls

Hen-and-chickens houseleek

Jovibarba sobolifera

Fl stem from rosette centre

Fl tubular, 1.7 cm

Dense lf rosette, basal plantlets joined by stolons; 6 hr-fringed ptls. *Ht:* 25 cm; *D:* C, E; *Fl:* 7–8

47

Saxifrage family Saxifragaceae

Herbs with alternate leaves. The symmetrical flowers usually have 5 petals and sepals, 5 or 10 stamens and two carpels which are joined at their base.

Meadow saxifrage

Saxifraga granulata

Ptls to 1.7 cm, 2–12 fls per infl

Rosette of *c.* 7 lvs, some long hrs; bulbils in lf axils. Fls have 10 stamens as all *Saxifraga* spp. *Ht:* 35 cm; *D:* N, C; *Fl:* 4–6

Mossy saxifrage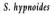

S. hypnoides

Mat-forming. Lvs 3–5 lobed with sharp points, narrow to stk; stem hrlss. Fl shs fine to 20 cm, ptls to 1 cm. *D:* NW; *Fl:* 5–7

Rue-leaved saxifrage

S. tridactylites

Upright to 15 cm, sticky hrs all over. Lvs 3–5 lobed, dense at base. Fls sol or in gps on long stks, ptls to 3 mm long. *D:* T (not far N); *Fl:* 4–6

Arctic saxifrage

S. nivalis

Ptls 3 mm, spls uprt or spread

Leaves to 2 cm, oval or spathulate, serrate, purple below in basal rosette. Infl dense, 3–12 fls, fl sh to 15 cm. *D:* N; *Fl:* 7–8

Drooping saxifrage

S. cernua

Ptls 1.3 cm

Basal lvs 3–5 lobed in rosette, top lvs unstkd, bulbils in axils. Fl shs unbranched, fl sol on bulbil gp. *Ht:* 10 cm; *D:* N, Alps; *Fl:* 7

48

Purple saxifrage

S. oppositifolia

Ptls *to 1 cm*

Perennial with long, prostrate branches. Erect shs only 1–2 cm tall. Dense lvs in 4 ranks. Fls sol on erect shs. *D:* N, S; *Fl:* 3–5

Yellow saxifrage | Starry saxifrage

S. aïzoides | ### *S. stellaris*

Perennial. Vegetative and flowering shs to 20 cm tall. Lvs linear, unstkd, dense. Fl shs hry, infl of 1–10 fls with lfy bracts, spls spread, ptls to 7 mm long. *D:* N, mts in S; *Fl:* 6–9

Basal lvs as *S. nivalis* (p 48) but green, few long hrs. Over 12 fls in infl, spls reflexed. *Ht:* 10 cm; *D:* T; *Fl:* 6–8

Opposite-leaved golden saxifrage | Alternate-leaved golden saxifrage

Chrysosplenium oppositifolium | ### *C. alternifolium*

Fl *has 4 or 5 spls, no ptls*

Stem lvs *alternate*

Prostrate rooting stems to 15 cm. Basal lvs round, narrow abruptly to short stk. *D:* T (not far N); *Fl:* 4–7

Very like *C. oppositifolium* but creeping shs lfless, basal lvs have notch at attachment to v long lf stk. *D:* T (not far N); *Fl:* 4–7

49

Grass of Parnassus family Parnassiaceae

Perennial herbs with undivided, alternate leaves. Terminal, solitary flowers have 5 sepals and petals, 5 true stamens plus 5 infertile structures and 4 fused carpels.

Grass of Parnassus

Parnassia palustris

Ptls *veined c. 1 cm*

Hairless herb to 30 cm. Lvs heart-shaped, untoothed to 3 cm, stks longer than blades. Fl stks vertical, single lf near base. *D:* T; *Fl:* 7–10

Rose family Rosaceae

Herbs, shrubs and trees with alternate leaves having stipules. The flowers have 5 petals and sepals (and sometimes an epicalyx), more than 5 stamens and from one to many carpels. The flower stalk is often involved in fruit formation.

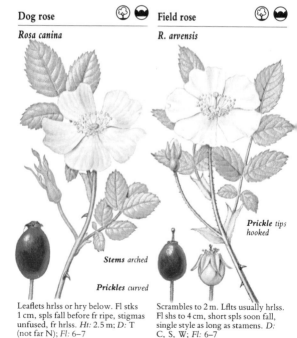

Dog rose

Rosa canina

Field rose

R. arvensis

Stems *arched*

Prickles *curved*

Prickle *tips hooked*

Leaflets hrlss or hry below. Fl stks 1 cm, spls fall before fr ripe, stigmas unfused, fr hrlss. *Ht:* 2.5 m; *D:* T (not far N); *Fl:* 6–7

Scrambles to 2 m. Lflts usually hrlss. Fl shs to 4 cm, short spls soon fall, single style as long as stamens. *D:* C, S, W; *Fl:* 6–7

50

Burnet rose

R. pimpinellifolia

Fr *dark*

Bush to 1 m. Straight prickles and stiff hrs on stems; 3–5 lflt prs. *D:* T (not Scand); *Fl:* 5–7

Downy rose

R. tomentosa

Prickles just curved; lvs have downy hrs; fl shs sticky, hry; spls fall. *Ht:* 1.5 m; *D:* T (not far N); *Fl:* 6–7

Alpine rose

R. pendulina

No prickles. Fls have long lf stks round shs, fl shs bend back in fr. *Ht:* 2 m; *D:* S mts, C; *Fl:* 6–7

Wild rose

R. stylosa

Fl *to 3 mm*

Lvs *hry below*

Arched shs 3 m, prickles hooked. Sticky hrs on fl shs; styles fused, separate in fr. *D:* W, S; *Fl:* 6–7

Sweet briar

R. rubiginosa

Stems uprt, hooked prickles vary in size; lflts have glands below. *Ht:* 1.5 m; *D:* T (not far N); *Fl:* 6–7

Provence rose

R. gallica

Fr *has sticky hrs*

Patch-forming. Lflts glaucous, round. Fls to 9 cm, frag, styles hry. *Ht:* 65 cm; *D:* C, S; *Fl:* 5–6

Creeping cinquefoil

Potentilla reptans

Prostrate, rts at nodes. Erect fl shs to 30 cm. Stipules untoothed. Fl has epicalyx as in all spp of *Potentilla*. *D:* T (not far N); *Fl:* 6–9

Silverweed

P. anserina

Creeping stolons to 1 m; 10 lflt prs, silky white hrs. Fls long-stkd, sol. *D:* T; *Fl:* 6–8

Shrubby cinquefoil

P. fruticosa

Ptls
to 1.2 cm

Lvs
untoothed

Shrub; lvs pinnate, 5-lobed. Fls in terminal infl. *Ht:* to 1 m; *D:* NW, mts in S; *Fl:* 6–7

Hoary cinquefoil

P. argentea

Lower lvs
5-lobed, v
hry below

Upright fl shs often hry. Fls to 1.5 cm, spls hry. *Ht:* 40 cm; *D:* N, Alps; *Fl:* 6–9

Tormentil

P. erecta

Prostrate shs from lf rosette. Fls 1 cm, only 4 spls and ptls. *Ht:* 40 cm; *D:* T; *Fl:* 6–9

Barren strawberry

P. sterilis

Fl to 1.5 cm

Softly hry to 15 cm, spread stolons, lvs not glossy, ptls far apart. *D:* W, S, C; *Fl:* 2–5

Marsh cinquefoil

P. palustris

Spls pointed

Has creeping rhizome. Lvs serrate, 5 or 7 lflts, spls purple. *Ht:* 35 cm; *D:* T; *Fl:* 5–7

Norwegian cinquefoil

P. norvegica

Leaves serrate, hry; fl shs erect, clustered fls, 5 hry spls. *Ht:* 40 cm; *D:* N, C, E; *Fl:* 6–9

Alpine cinquefoil

Potentilla crantzii

Fl large to 2.5 cm

Lower lvs 5-lobed, hry, especially below; fl shs in lf axils, spls hry. *Ht:* 20 cm; *D:* N, S; *Fl:* 6–7

Sibbaldia

Sibbaldia procumbens

Lvs 3-lobed

Stems have flat hrs

Tussocky. Infl dense, fls 5 mm, spls pointed, ptls v small or absent. *Ht:* 2 cm; *D:* N, S; *Fl:* 7–8

Hautbois strawberry

Fragaria moschata

Lflts short-stkd

Robust spread hrs on fl shs, fls 2 cm. Achenes on fr, but none near base. *Ht:* 30 cm; *D:* C, W; *Fl:* 4–7

Wild strawberry

F. vesca

Fl stks have flat hrs above

Lvs glossy above

Like *Potentilla sterilis* (p 52) but no gaps between ptls; achenes all over fr. *Ht:* 20 cm; *D:* T; *Fl:* 4–7

Stone bramble

Rubus saxatilis

Infl dense

Fr of 2–6 parts

Prostrate, uprt fl shs 35 cm; lvs 3-lobed (unlike *R. chamaemorus*). *D:* T; *Fl:* 6–8

Arctic bramble

R. arcticus

Fl has 5–7 ptls

No prickles; 3-lobed lvs; infl long-stkd, 1–3 fls, many fr parts. *Ht:* 20 cm; *D:* N; *Fl:* 7–9

Bramble

R. fruticosus

Curved prickles; fr of 20+ parts, no bloom (unlike *R. caesius*). *Ht:* 1.5 m *D:* T; *Fl:* 5–9

Water avens

Geum rivale

Hairy. Top lft large. Fls nodding, spls purple, styles persist in fr. *Ht:* 45 cm; *D:* T; *Fl:* 5–9

Alpine avens

G. montanum

Rhizomatous. Top lflt round. Fls 3 cm, often 6 ptls, feathery fr. *Ht:* 7 cm; *D:* C, S; *Fl:* 7–8

Herb bennet

G. urbanum

Basal lvs pinnate

Stem lvs simple above, lobed lower down. Fls uprt, spls green. *Ht:* 45 cm; *D:* T (not far N); *Fl:* 6–8

Mountain avens

Dryas octopetala

Fl stks long, fls sol

Many v hry lvs; 7–10 ptls, sticky black hrs on spls, feathery fr. *Ht:* 6 cm; *D:* S mts, N; *Fl:* 6–7

Lady's mantle

Alchemilla vulgaris

Large lvs, lobes half radius, green below; no ptls. *Ht:* 30 cm; *D:* W, C; *Fl:* 6–9

Alpine lady's mantle

Alchemilla alpina

Lvs to 3.5 cm, silky below

Creeping; lf blades cut almost to centre; fls 3 mm. *Ht:* 15 cm; *D:* N, W; *Fl:* 6–8

Agrimony

Agrimonia eupatoria

Infl a spike

Hairy, hooked spines on fls persist in fr. *Ht:* 60 cm; *D:* T (not far N); *Fl:* 6–8

Meadowsweet

Filipendula ulmaria
Infl dense

Leaves pinnate, 2–5 big lflts alt with small prs; 5 ptls, fr spirally twisted. *Ht:* 1 m; *D:* T; *Fl:* 6–9

Great burnet

Sanguisorba officinalis

Lflts toothed

Pinnate lvs, 3–7 prs lflts; 4 red spls, no ptls, 4 stms; ♂, ♀ parts in same fl. *Ht:* 80 cm; *D:* T; *Fl:* 6–9

Salad burnet

S. minor
Basal lvs have 4–12 lflt prs

Basal lvs have 4–12 lflt prs

Scrambles to 60 cm; 4 green spls, no ptls, many stms; ♂ fls atop round infl, ♀ below. *D:* W, C; *Fl:* 5–8

Dropwort

F. vulgaris

Basal lvs jagged, 8–20 prs large lflts between small prs; 6 ptls. *Ht:* 60 cm; *D:* T (not N); *Fl:* 5–8

Parsley piert

Aphanes arvensis

Creeps to 20 cm. Lvs have 3 lobed lflts. Fls v small with only spls and stipules. *D:* W, C; *Fl:* 4–10

Goat's beard spiraea

Aruncus dioicus

Lvs to 1 m

Rhizomatous. Fl shs to 2 m; lvs 2× cut, serrate. Infl pyramidal, fls unstkd. *D:* C mts; *Fl:* 6–8

55

Pea family Leguminosae

Compound leaves have stipules and maybe tendrils. Flowers have an erect (standard) petal, two wing petals and two petals joined into a keel; 5 sepals form a tube. The fruit is a pod.

Red clover

Trifolium pratense

Erect or straggling per. Lvs have 3 lflts, often with pale V mark. Stipules contracted to a fine point. Fls in dense globular heads. Forage crop. *Ht:* 30 cm; *D:* T; *Fl:* 5–9

Zig-zag clover

T. medium

Straggling per. Like *T. pratense* but lflts narrower and stipules oblong. Fl head arises from a pair of lvs. *Ht:* 30 cm; *D:* T; *Fl:* 6–9

Mountain clover

T. montanum

Hairy per like *T. hybridum*. Lflts to 4 cm long, elliptical. Fl heads often paired on v long, hry stks. *Ht:* to 60 cm; *D:* C, S; *Fl:* 5–7

White clover

T. repens

Creeping hrlss per, roots at nodes. Lflts broader near tip, white V mark, stipules oval. Spls short-toothed. *Ht:* 30 cm; *D:* T; *Fl:* 6–9

Haresfoot clover

T. arvense

Softly hry ann. Brs straggling, hry. Infl cylindrical, downy, long-stkd. Ptls half spl length. *Ht:* 10 cm; *D:* T (not far N); *Fl:* 6–9

Alsike clover

T. hybridum

Erect per. Lflts elliptic. Stipules oval, long, fine points. Teeth on spl tube 2 × tube length. Infl long-stkd. *Ht:* 40 cm; *D:* T; *Fl:* 6–9

Lesser yellow trefoil

T. dubium

Infl of up to 26 fls

Standard ptl folds round fr unlike *T. campestre* (hop trefoil). *Ht:* 15 cm; *D:* T (not far N); *Fl:* 5–10

Strawberry clover

T. fragiferum

Lflts serrated. Spls inflate round fr swelling head. *Ht:* 20 cm; *D:* T (not far N); *Fl:* 7–9

Sulphur clover

T. ochroleucon

Hairy per; lflts to 3 cm, 2 unstkd lvs round fl head; 1 v long spl tooth. *Ht:* 30 cm; *D:* W, C, S; *Fl:* 6–7

Fenugreek

T. ornithopodioides

Delicate hrlss ann. Stipules lance-shaped. Infl has 1–3 short stkd fls. Fr curved. *Ht:* 10 cm; *D:* T; *Fl:* 5–9

Birdsfoot trefoil

Lotus corniculatus

Infl of 2–6 fls

 *Pods twist spirally when split*

Scrambling hrlss per. Stems solid. Lvs have 5 lflts. Infl horseshoe shaped. *Ht:* 20 cm; *D:* T; *Fl:* 6–9

Suffocated clover

T. suffocatum

Prostrate, hrlss ann. Lflts toothed, triangular, to 5 mm, stipules pointed. Infls at sh tips, dense unstkd. *Ht:* 5 cm; *D:* S, W; *Fl:* 4–8

Marsh birdsfoot trefoil

L. uliginosus

Erect or climbing per, sometimes hry. Stem hollow. Lflts to 2 cm. Infl with 5–12 fls on long, slim stks. *Ht:* 40 cm; *D:* W, C, S; *Fl:* 6–8

Dragon's teeth

Tetragonolobus maritimus

Like *Lotus* but lvs short-stkd, 3-lobed, big stipules; fls sol. *Ht:* 20 cm; *D:* C, S; *Fl:* 5–7

Bush vetch

V. sepium

Lflts in 5–9 prs

Trailing, hrlss to 1 m with tendrils; 2–6 fls in infl, spl teeth not equal. *D:* T; *Fl:* 5–8

Upright vetch

V. orobus

Fr to 3 cm

Has 6–9 lflt prs, no tendrils, toothed stipules; infl 6–20 fls. *Ht:* 30 cm; *D:* W; *Fl:* 6–9

Birdsfoot

Ornithopus perpusillus

Prostrate, hry; 4–13 lflt prs, lowest near stem. Infl of 3–6 fls; fruit constricted. *Ht:* 35 cm; *D:* W, C; *Fl:* 5–8

Wood vetch

V. sylvatica

Infl 6–18 fls

Scrambling, hrlss, has tendrils; 6–9 lflt prs, stipules toothed; top spl teeth short. *Ht:* 1 m; *D:* N, C, E; *Fl:* 6–8

Common vetch

Vicia sativa

Fr to 8 cm

Lflts in 4–8 prs

Scrambling with tendrils; dark spot on stipules. Fls in 1s or 2s, spl teeth equal. *Ht:* 1 m; *D:* T; *Fl:* 5–9

Tufted vetch

V. cracca

Tendrils present

Clambers to 2 m; 8–12 lflt prs; infl 10–14 fls, top spl teeth short. *D:* T; *Fl:* 6–8

Yellow vetch

V. lutea

Prostrate, hrlss; 3–7 lflt prs, triangular stipules, has tendrils; fls sol, fr hry. *Ht:* 50 cm; *D:* S, W; *Fl:* 6–8

Hairy tare

V. hirsuta

Scrambles to 70 cm. Lflts narrow, tendrils present, stipules 4-lobed; infl 1–9 fls, fr hry. *D:* T; *Fl:* 5–8

Fl to 2.5 cm

Lflts in 4–8 prs

Kidney vetch

Anthyllis vulneraria

Prostrate or uprt; lflts oval, top one v large. Infl dense, woolly spls, fls 1.5 cm. *Ht:* 50 cm; *D:* T; *Fl:* 6–9

Yellow milk vetch

Oxytropis campestris

Hairy; 10–15 lflt prs; infl oval, 5–15 fls, keel fine pointed as in all *Oxytropis* spp. *Ht:* 15 cm; *D:* N, S; *Fl:* 6–8

Hairy milk vetch

O. pilosa

Robust, v hry per to 50 cm; 5–15 lflt prs with flat hrs. Oval infl, many fls, narrow fr with spread hrs. *D:* C, E; *Fl:* 6–8

Mountain milk vetch

O. halleri

Softly hry; 8–18 lflt prs; infl oval with 5–15 fls, keel has a long tooth *c.* 1 mm. Flat hrs on fr. *Ht:* to 30 cm; *D:* C, S; *Fl:* 6–7

Purple milk vetch

Astragalus danicus

L flts in 6–13 prs

Delicate per, silky hrs. Fl sh to 2 × lf length; fr 2-celled. *Ht:* 25 cm; *D:* T; *Fl:* 5–7

Wild lentil

A. cicer

L flts in 10–15 prs

Scrambling. Fl shs just shorter than lvs. Spl teeth half tube length. *Ht:* 65 cm; *D:* C; *Fl:* 6–7

Wild liquorice

A. glycophyllos

Plant nearly hrlss

Straggles to 1.5 m. Only 4–7 lflt prs. Fl shs under half lf length, fr curved. *D:* T; *Fl:* 5–8

Alpine milk vetch

A. alpinus

L flts in 7–12 prs

Prostrate; lflts hrlss above. Loose infl, 5–15 fls, spls hry. *Ht:* 30 cm; *D:* N, S; *Fl:* 7–8

Yellow alpine milk vetch

A. frigidus

L fls oval in 3–8 prs

L fls oval in 3–8 prs

Erect, hrlss; loose infl, 5–20 fls, teeth on spl tube triangular. *Ht:* 35 cm; *D:* N, S; *Fl:* 7–8

Norwegian milk vetch

A. norvegicus

Erect, hrlss; 6–7 lflt prs. Fl shs 2 × length of lvs; fr flat, oval. *Ht:* 30 cm; *D:* T; *Fl:* 7–8

Crown vetch	Scorpion vetch	Lesser scorpion vetch

Crown vetch
Coronilla varia

Scorpion vetch
C. coronata

Lesser scorpion vetch
C. minima

Ptls 1 cm

Infl long-stkd

Fr 4-angled

Spreading, hrlss; 7–12 lft prs. Long-stkd infl, 10–20 fls. *Ht:* 1 m; *D:* T; *Fl:* 5–8

Fr to 3 cm

Stout, glaucous; 3–7 lft prs; infl 12–20 fls; fr 4-angled. *Ht:* 60 cm; *D:* C; *Fl:* 5–7

Woody per. Leaflets unstkd, 2–6 prs. Infl of up to 15 fls, ptls to 8 mm, Pod 4-angled to 3.5 cm. *Ht:* 30 cm; *D:* SW; *Fl:* 4–6

Small scorpion vetch
C. vaginalis

Scorpion senna
C. emerus

Horseshoe vetch
Hippocrepis comosa

Ptls to 1 cm

Fls 1 cm long

Woody per to 50 cm. Oval, short-stkd lflts in 2–6 prs. Infl of 4–6 fls; pod to 3 cm long has 6 angles and 4 wings. *D:* C; *Fl:* 5–6

Has 2–4 prs glaucous fine-pointed lflts, infl 2–6 fls, fr hangs. *Ht:* 80 cm; *D:* C; *Fl:* 4–6

Hairless, to 40 cm, woody base; lflts 4–5, obovate. Fl sh long, infl of 5–8 flowers, fruit has horseshoe-shaped parts. *D:* W, C; *Fl:* 5–7

Meadow vetchling

Lathyrus pratensis

Clambers, angled shs, fine hrs; 1 pr pointed lflts, a tendril and arrow-shaped stipules. Fl stk long, fr flat. *Ht:* 1 m; *D:* T; *Fl:* 5–8

Yellow vetchling

L. aphaca

Hairless, to 1 m. No lflts but triangular stipules to 3 cm. Fls sol, long-stkd, long spl teeth, fr curved. *D:* W, C, S; *Fl:* 6–8

Grass vetchling

L. nissolia

Plant *hrlss*

Erect to 90 cm; no lflts or tendrils but has grass-like shs. *D:* W, C, S; *Fl:* 5–7

Spring pea

L. vernus

Fls *to 2 cm*

Plant *perennial*

Erect, usually hrlss. Stem angled, 2–4 lflt prs, no tendrils; infl 3–10 spaced fls, fr hrlss. *Ht:* 50 cm; *D:* T (not GB); *Fl:* 4–6

Narrow-leaved everlasting pea

L. sylvestris

Bushy, hrlss, winged stem; 1 lflt pr, single tendril; stipules thin, spread. Infl 3–8 fls, fr winged. *Ht:* 1.5 m; *D:* T (not N); *Fl:* 6–8

Bitter vetchling

L. montanus

Tendrils *absent*

Rhizomatous. Winged stem. Lflts narrow, 2–4 prs. Infl 2–8 fls, flat hrs on flower shs and spls. *Ht:* 30 cm; *D:* S, W, C; *Fl:* 6–7

Marsh pea

L. palustris

Lvs have narrow stipules

Stems winged

Scrambles to 1.2 m; 2–3 lflt prs and branched tendril per lf. Infl of 2–6 fls; fr flat. *D:* T; *Fl:* 5–7

Tuberous pea

L. tuberosus

Has rt tubers, stem angled; lvs have 1 lflt pr, 1 tendril; fr cylindrical. *Ht:* 1 m; *D:* T (not N); *Fl:* 6–7

Sea pea

L. japonicus

Lflts broad, elliptic

Lflts in 3–4 prs

Low per, angled shs to 90 cm; has tendrils, stipules triangular, infl 5–15 fls, fr rigid. *D:* W, N; *Fl:* 6–8

Goat's rue

Galega officinalis

Stout, uprt; 4–8 lflt prs, arrow-shaped stipules. Fl shs equal lvs; fr straight. *D:* E, C, S; *Fl:* 6–7

Common melilot

Melilotus officinalis

Fl has short keel

Sprawling or uprt; many 6 mm fls, fr ribbed, hrlss, brown. *Ht:* 2 m; *D:* T; *Fl:* 7–9

White melilot

M. alba

Infl loose

Keel and wing ptls shorter than standard; fr hrlss, brown. *Ht:* 1 m; *D:* T; *Fl:* 7–8

Tall melilot

M. altissima

Like *M. officinalis* but to 1.5 m. All ptls equal; fr hry, black. *D:* T (not E); *Fl:* 6–8

63

Bladder senna

Colutea arborescens

Fl to 2 cm

Lflts in 3–6 prs

Shrubby, v branched; lvs pinnate, stipules pointed. Infl of 3–8 fls, fr inflated. *Ht:* 4 m; *D:* S; *Fl:* 5–7

Spotted medick

Medicago arabica

Lflts heart-shaped

Prostrate, hrlss; lflts toothed, in 3s, black blotch; 1–4 fls in infl; fr coiled. *Ht:* 45 cm; *D:* S, W; *Fl:* 4–8

Black medick

M. lupulina

Infl dense, long-stkd

Prostrate. Lflt tips notched with projecting nerve. Fr curled. *Ht:* 35 cm; *D:* T (not far N); *Fl:* 4–8

Sickle medick

M. falcata

Lflts narrow to 1.5 cm

Scrambling. Infl loose, each fl on sh longer than spls, fr curved. *Ht:* 50 cm; *D:* T (not N); *Fl:* 6–8

Rest harrow

Ononis repens

Creeping, no spines but sticky hrs; fl wings equal keel. *Ht:* 45 cm; *D:* W, C; *Fl:* 6–9

Small rest harrow

O. reclinata

Fls to 7 mm

Stems slender

Sticky, uprt, no spines. Lflts v hry, fl shs bend back in fr. *Ht:* 7 cm; *D:* S, W; *Fl:* 6–7

Hairy rest harrow

O. pusilla

Lflts toothed

Erect, hry, woody base. Fls unstkd, spls and ptls 1 cm. *Ht:* 20 cm; *D:* S; *Fl:* 6–8

Spiny rest harrow

Ononis spinosa

Large yellow rest harrow

Ononis natrix

Sainfoin

Onobrychis viciifolia

Pod *hry*

Lflts in 6–12 prs

Woody uprt stems spiny with 2 lines of hrs; keel ptls longer than wings. *Ht:* 45 cm; *D:* W, C; *Fl:* 6–9

Dwarf shrub, stickily hry. Lvs variable oval to narrow; infl loose, ptls veined. *Ht:* 45 cm; *D:* S, W; *Fl:* 5–8

Upright per; pinnate lvs, lflts narrow with pointed tips. Loose infl, to 50 fls. *Ht:* 60 cm; *D:* T; *Fl:* 6–8

Hedysarum

Hedysarum hedysaroides

Star-fruited fenugreek

Trigonella monspeliaca

Classical fenugreek

T. foenum-graecum

Fr 1 cm

Lflts oval, blunt in 3–10 prs

Hairless; lvs pinnate; infl of 15–35 fls each 2 cm, colour varies. Drooping fr has a flange. *Ht:* 30 cm; *D:* S, C; *Fl:* 7–8

Prostrate, hry; lvs 3-lobed, lflts obovate; fls 4 mm, unstkd, gps of 4–14. Fr just curved, hanging. *Ht:* 25 cm; *D:* C, S; *Fl:* 3–6

Erect, sparsely hry. Lflts narrow, fine-toothed; fls short-stkd in prs in lf axils, fr curved. *Ht:* 35 cm; *D:* C, S; *Fl:* 4–5

65

Petty whin

Genista anglica

Fl 8 mm

Shrub with spines to 2 cm, some curved; lvs hrlss, no stipules; spl tube 2-lipped. *Ht:* 45 cm; *D:* W; *Fl:* 5–6

Broom

Cytisus scoparius

Pod 3 cm, hry

Fl stk 1 cm, hry

Erect hry shrub to 2 m, stems ridged; lvs 3-lobed, fall easily. Fl 2 cm. *D:* W, S, C; *Fl:* 5–6

Winged broom

Chamaespartium sagittale

Mat-forming, fl shs broad-winged, lvs hry below, infl dense. *Ht:* 40 cm; *D:* C; *Fl:* 5–9

German greenweed

G. germanica

Lvs hry below

Spiny, hry shrub to 60 cm. Infl loose, spls and fl shs very hairy, standard ptl pointed at tip. *D:* SW; *Fl:* 5–9

Clustered broom

Chamaecytisus supinus

Fl to 2.5 cm

Fr 3 cm

Hairy but no spines; lvs 3-lobed. Infl of 2–8 fls, spls hry. *Ht:* 70 cm; *D:* C, S; *Fl:* 5–7

Dyer's greenweed

G. tinctoria

Fl 1.5 cm

Fr flat

Woody, uprt, no spines; shs grooved. Lvs hry at edges; infl long. *Ht:* 60 cm; *D:* T (not far N); *Fl:* 7–9

Black broom

Lembotropis nigricans

Fls to 1 cm

Fr 3 cm

Lflts dark above

Erect shrub, no spines. Long infl of drooping buds and fls. *Ht:* 1 m; *D:* C, S; *Fl:* 6–7

Gorse	Western dwarf gorse	Dwarf gorse

Ulex europaeus

U. gallii

U. minor

Plant *rather prostrate*

Shrub, many ridged spines to 2 cm, young plants have 3-lobed lvs. Spls hry. *Ht:* 1.5 m; *D:* W; *Fl:* 2–6

Hairy; unfurrowed spines *c.* 2 cm. Spls ⅔ ptl length, wings longer than keel. *Ht:* 60 cm; *D:* W; *Fl:* 7–9

Spines *c.* 1 cm, not furrowed. Spls as long as ptls, wings as long as keel. *Ht:* to 1 m; *D:* W; *Fl:* 7–9

Wood sorrel family Oxalidaceae

Herbs with a fleshy rootstock and often alternate, palmate leaves. The solitary or sparsely grouped flowers have 5 petals and sepals and 10 stamens. The fruit is a capsule.

Wood sorrel

Yellow oxalis

Oxalis acetosella

O. corniculata

Lf stks *long, thin*

Stems *hry, rooting*

Stk *of each fl c. 1 cm*

Creeping rhizomatous per. Lvs 3-lobed, lflts to 2 cm. Fls sol, to 3 cm on long thin stks. Fr to 4 mm. *Ht:* 10 cm; *D:* T; *Fl:* 4–6

Weak, prostrate. Lvs 3-lobed with small stipules, lflts deeply cut at tips. Long-stkd infl of 1–6 fls. *Ht:* 10 cm; *D:* S; *Fl:* 6–9

Geranium family Geraniaceae

Herbs or shrubs having alternate, lobed or compound leaves with stipules. Flowers have 5 separate petals and 5 sepals in a tube which persists round the long-beaked fruit.

Bloody cranesbill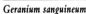

Geranium sanguineum

Meadow cranesbill

G. pratense

Bushy herb with creeping rhizome. Lvs in narrow segments with flat white hrs. Fls sol, to 3.6 cm, fr to 3 cm. *Ht:* 25 cm; *D:* T; *Fl:* 7–8

Perennial. Erect hry stems. Lvs have deeply cut lobes. Paired fls on long stks which bend back in fr. Fr *c.* 2.5 cm. *Ht:* 50 cm; *D:* T; *Fl:* 6–9

Hedgerow cranesbill

G. pyrenaicum

Shining cranesbill

G. lucidum

Fl to 2 cm

Fr beak 1 cm

Perennial with many sticky hrs. Fls in pairs. Fr stks bent back but tips erect. *Ht:* 40 cm; *D:* S, W; *Fl:* 6–8

Annual branched from ground. Lvs glossy, reddish, cut to half lf width. Fls on spread, up-curved stks. *Ht:* 25 cm; *D:* T (not NE); *Fl:* 5–8

Herb Robert

G. robertianum

Ptls to 1.2 cm

Wood cranesbill

G. sylvaticum

Ptls to 1.8 cm

Biennial or ann. Shoots much-branched, delicate, reddish. Lvs lobed, lobes divided. Fl stks uprt. *Ht:* 30 cm; *D:* T (not far N); *Fl:* 5–9

Perennial. Stems have sticky hrs above. Lvs hry, 7-lobed. Fls in pairs. Fl stks erect in fruit. *Ht:* 50 cm; *D:* T; *Fl:* 6–7

Long-stalked cranesbill

G. columbinum

Fl stks long

Branching ann. Flat hrs on stems and spl veins. Fr hrlss. *Ht:* 30 cm; *D:* T (not far N); *Fl:* 6–7

Dove's foot cranesbill

G. molle

Annual covered with soft white hrs. Lvs round. *Ht:* 30 cm; *D:* T (not far N); *Fl:* 4–9

Cut-leaved cranesbill

G. dissectum

Ptls to 5 mm

Straggling. Hrs on shs down-pointed, on spls sticky. *Ht:* 40 cm; *D:* T (not far N); *Fl:* 5–8

Marsh cranesbill

G. palustre

Ptls unnotched

Hairy per. Lvs toothed. Few fls in infl. Fr stks bend back. *Ht:* 40 cm; *D:* T (not N); *Fl:* 7–8

Common storksbill

Erodium cicutarium

Fls to 9 per cluster

Hairy. Lvs compound, lflts cut. Ptls longer than spls. *Ht:* 30 cm; *D:* T; *Fl:* 6–9

Soft storksbill

E. malacoides

Flowers in gps of 3–7. Sticky hrs on fl stks and spls. *Ht:* 30 cm; *D:* SW; *Fl:* 2–6

Sea storksbill

E. maritimum

Ptls to 4 mm

Flat ann. Hrs bristly. Lvs lobed to half width. Fls sol or paired. *D:* NW; *Fl:* 5–9

Musk storksbill

E. moschatum

Plant smells of musk

Annual, many white hrs. Ptls just longer than spls. *Ht:* 30 cm; *D:* S, W; *Fl:* 5–7

Flax family Linaceae

Herbs with simple, usually alternate leaves without stipules. The flowers usually have 5 petals, sepals and stamens and an ovary with 3–5 cells. The fruit is a capsule that splits vertically.

Perennial flax

Linum perenne

Hairless perennial with rigid, upright stems. Numerous alternate leaves 1–2 cm long. Spls rounded, less than half fr length, ptls to 2 cm. Fr stks erect. A variable sp. *Ht:* 45 cm; *D:* C, E; *Fl:* 6–7

Pale flax

L. bienne

Hairless ann or per; stems uprt, branched. Ptls to 1.2 cm, spls oval, pointed tips, more than half fr length. Ancestor of cultivated flax. *Ht:* 45 cm; *D:* W, S; *Fl:* 5–9

Purging flax

L. catharticum

Delicate ann, slender stems. Lvs opposite, oval, rounded to 1.2 cm. Many fls in loose infl, fl shs fine, ptls 6 mm, spls pointed. Fr 3 mm, same length as spls. Seeds purgative. *Ht:* 15 cm; *D:* T; *Fl:* 6–9

Yellow flax

L. flavum

Ptls *c. 2 cm*

Lvs *to 3 cm*

Robust per. Erect shs from dense base. Lvs broadest near tip. Infl branched 20–40 clustered flowers pointed spls with hry edges. Spls just longer than fr. *Ht:* 45 cm; *D:* C, S; *Fl:* 5–8

Allseed

Radiola linoides

Tiny ann to 8 cm. Stems slender, branched, bushy. Lvs opp, 3 mm long. Fls *c.* 2 mm across in flat-topped clusters have 4 ptls and spls. Fr spherical, *c.* 1 mm diam. *D:* T (not NE); *Fl:* 7–8

Spurge family Euphorbiaceae

Annual or perennial herbs with alternate leaves. Male and female flowers are usually separate but may be grouped together in a cup-like structure. The ovary has two or three cells.

Sea spurge

Euphorbia paralias

Lvs to 2 cm

Stiff, hrlss, glaucous per; erect usually unbranched stems. Thick fleshy lvs have obscure midrib below. Fls in terminal clusters, ♂ and ♀ joined in a cup. Fr hrlss. *Ht:* to 40 cm; *D:* W, S; *Fl:* 8–11

Purple spurge

E. peplis

Prostrate ann, usually with 4 main branches from base. Lvs to 1 cm, enlarged on one side at base and with divided stipules. Infl to 2 mm long, fr a hairless, 3-sided capsule. *Ht:* 4 cm; *D:* T; *Fl:* 7–9

Wood spurge

E. amygdaloides

Robust, hry per to 80 cm. Lvs on veg shs taper to stk at base, lvs on fl shs do not. Infl a 5–10 rayed umbel with kidney-shaped bracts below. *D:* NW, C, S; *Fl:* 3–5

Portland spurge

E. portlandica

Like a small version of *E. paralias* but stems unbranched. Lvs fleshy, prominent midrib below, tapered to base. Often reddens with age. *Ht:* 25 cm; *D:* W; *Fl:* 5–9

Dwarf spurge

E. exigua

Hairless, glaucous, to 30 cm. Lvs to 3 cm, untoothed, narrow, tips pointed. Infl an umbel with 3 rays, bracts below lvs broader than true lvs. *D:* T (not E); *Fl:* 6–10

Petty spurge

Euphorbia peplus

Hairless ann, stem simple or branched. Lvs to 3 cm, oval, untoothed. Infl a 3-rayed umbel with stklss bracts. *Ht:* 30 cm; *D:* T; *Fl:* 4–11

Sun spurge

E. helioscopia

Lvs blunt, rounded, toothed near tip

Hairless, uprt, few brs. Infl 5-rayed, bracts round at base. *Ht:* 35 cm; *D:* T; *Fl:* 5–10

Caper spurge

Euphorbia lathyris

Lvs to 2 cm

Glaucous, hrlss; lvs opp, broad, round at base. Infl 2–6 brs, fr to 2 cm. *Ht:* 1 m; *D:* S, W, C; *Fl:* 6–7

Annual mercury

Mercurialis annua

Near hrlss; erect shs v branched; lvs stkd. ♂ and ♀ plants separate, ♂ fls in spike, ♀ sol, unstkd. *Ht:* 40 cm; *D:* T; *Fl:* 7–10

Dog's mercury

M. perennis

Lvs to 8 cm, short-stkd

Patch-forming, hry. Shs uprt, no brs. ♂ and ♀ plants separate, ♂ fls clustered, stkd, ♀ sol, long-stkd. *Ht:* 30 cm; *D:* T; *Fl:* 2–4

Cypress spurge

E. cyparissias

Lvs narrow to 3 cm

Has rhizome; dense shs hrlss, often branched. Many alt lvs. Infl of 5–9 brs. *Ht:* 20 cm; *D:* T (not far N); *Fl:* 5–8

Rue family Rutaceae

Herbs or shrubs with glandular leaves. The flowers have 4–5 free sepals and petals, 8 or 10 stamens and free styles.

Rue

Ruta graveolens

Strong-smelling hrlss per to 45 cm. Lower lvs stkd, v divided. Infl loose, spls narrow, pointed, ptls toothed. *D:* S, SC; *Fl:* 5–7

Milkwort family Polygalaceae

Herbs with simple leaves with no stipules. Asymmetrical flowers have 5 sepals (two petal-like) and 3–5 petals.

Common milkwort

Polygala vulgaris

Infl *loose, fls to 8 mm*

Scrambling stems, lvs narrow, alt to 1 cm at base, 3 cm above. Colour variable. *Ht:* 20 cm; *D:* T; *Fl:* 5–9

Chalk milkwort

P. calcarea

Prostrate per. Lvs in rosette to 2 cm, glossy, obovate, top lvs smaller. *Ht:* 15 cm; *D:* W; *Fl:* 5–7

Shrubby milkwort

P. chamaebuxus

Lvs *to 3 cm*

Dwarf shrub to 15 cm. Lvs oval or linear; fls sol or in prs, long-keeled. *D:* WC, S; *Fl:* 4–9

Thyme-leaved milkwort

P. serpyllifolia

Infl *of 3–8 fls*

Like *P. vulgaris* but lower lvs in opp prs, upper alt. More compact infl. *Ht:* 20 cm; *D:* W, C; *Fl:* 5–8

Balsam family Balsaminaceae

Herbs with no stipules at their leaf bases. The flowers have 3 or 5 sepals which are often petal-like and 5 petals, the upper one large and the lower ones united in two pairs. The ovary develops into a 5-celled, many-seeded fruit.

Himalayan balsam

Impatiens glandulifera

Erect, robust annual 1–2 m high. Stem stout, translucent and reddish. Leaves opposite or in groups of 3 around stem, stalked and sharply toothed. Flowers to 4 cm across with short, bent spurs and 3 sepals borne in groups of 5–10 at shoot tips. *D:* T; *Fl:* 7–10

Touch-me-not balsam

I. noli-tangere

Upright hrlss ann. Lvs to 12 cm stkd with teeth to 3 mm. Fls to 4 cm grouped in lf axils have 3 spls, the lowest with a curved spur. Name comes from seeds which shoot out if fruit is touched. *Ht:* 40 cm; *D:* T (not far N); *Fl:* 7–9

Orange balsam

I. capensis

Like *I. noli-tangere* but lvs to 8 cm with fewer smaller teeth. Fl spur curved. *Ht:* to 80 cm; *D:* W; *Fl:* 6–8

Small balsam

I. parviflora

Annual to 1 m. Lvs alternate with many teeth. Fls *c.* 1 cm, spur straight. *D:* T (not Scand); *Fl:* 7–11

Mallow family Malvaceae

Herbs and shrubs with leaves often palmately lobed. Grouped or single flowers have 5 free petals and 5 sepals either free or joined and often with an extra outer sepal whorl (epicalyx).

Common mallow

Malva sylvestris

Hairy perennial herb. Basal lvs rounded, lobed to 10 cm across. Fls to 4 cm in diam, clustered in lf axils. Epicalyx has 3 oval lobes. *Ht:* to 90 cm; *D:* T (not far N); *Fl:* 6–9

Dwarf mallow

M. neglecta

Often prostrate. Lvs to 7 cm diam. Epicalyx 3-lobed. *Ht:* 40 cm; *D:* T (not far N); *Fl:* 6–9

Rough mallow

A. hirsuta

Stem covered with sticky hrs. Lvs to 4 cm. Fls to 3 cm on long stks. Epicalyx 6-lobed. *Ht:* 40 cm; *D:* S; *Fl:* 6–7

Musk mallow

M. moschata

Leaves deeply cut. Fls sol to 6 cm. Epicalyx 3-lobed. *Ht:* 60 cm; *D:* T (not N); *Fl:* 7–8

Marsh mallow

Althaea officinalis

Softly hry. Short-stkd fls to 4 cm. Epicalyx 6-lobed. *Ht:* 1 m; *D:* T (not N); *Fl:* 8–9

Thymelaea family Thymelaeaceae

Shrubs with alternate, unlobed leaves with no stipules. Flowers have 4 or 5 lobed sepals placed at the end of the enlarged, tube-shaped, petal-like flower stalks.

Spurge laurel

Daphne laureola

Mezereon

D. mezereum

Annual thymelaea

Thymelaea passerina

Lvs hrlss to 10 cm

Fl to 1.2 cm

Lvs to 1.4 cm

Lvs to 15 cm, glossy

Evergreen, shs erect, lvs clustered at tips; fls 1 cm, 8 stamens, 4 spls, infl 5–10 fls; fr 1.2 cm, black. *Ht:* 70 cm; *D:* S, W; *Fl:* 2–4

Erect, decid. Gps of 2–4 fls appear before lvs over old lf scars; 4 spls equal tube in length; fr 1 cm, red. *Ht:* 65 cm; *D:* C, S; *Fl:* 2–4

Erect, hrlss. Gps of 1–3 fls to 4 mm in lf axils with 2 tiny bracts and tuft of hrs, spls blunt. *Ht:* 35 cm; *D:* S, W, C; *Fl:* 7–10

St John's wort family Guttiferae

Herbs or shrubs with simple opposite leaves often with resinous glands. The flowers have 5 petals and sepals and many stamens.

Perforate St John's wort

Hypericum perforatum

Fl 2 cm

Lvs elliptic, stklss, to 2 cm

Shs have 2 raised lines

Erect, hrlss. Lvs show translucent glands if held to light. Spls half ptl length, no black glands at edge. *Ht:* 70 cm; *D:* T (not far N); *Fl:* 6–9

Slender St John's wort

H. pulchrum

 Shs uprt **Lvs to 1 cm**

Translucent glands on lvs; spls round, under half ptl length, black glands at edge. *Ht:* 45 cm; *D:* NW; *Fl:* 6–8

Hairy St John's wort

H. hirsutum

Fl 1.5 cm

Shs uprt

Hairy, few brs; infl of many fls, spls half ptl length have black glands. *Ht:* 70 cm; *D:* T (not NE); *Fl:* 7–8

Trailing St John's wort

H. humifusum

Spls almost equal ptls

Prostrate per, delicate stems to 20 cm, 2 raised lines; translucent glands on lvs. Few 1 cm fls in infl, spl size varies. *D:* W, C; *Fl:* 6–9

Marsh St John's wort

H. elodes

Fl 1.5 cm

Very hry, few fls in infl, spls fine-toothed, stamens in 3 gps. *Ht:* 20 cm; *D:* W; *Fl:* 6–9

Tutsan

H. androsaemum

 Fl 2 cm

Stem has 2 lines; spls unequal, stamens long, fr a berry. *Ht:* 70 cm; *D:* W; *Fl:* 6–8

Square-stemmed St John's wort

H. tetrapterum

Upright, hrlss per, stems 4-ridged, lvs to 2 cm. Many 1 cm fls in infl, spls narrow, pointed, ⅔ ptl length. *Ht:* 55 cm; *D:* T (not far N); *Fl:* 6–9

77

Violet family Violaceae

Herbs whose leaves have stipules. Often spurred, solitary flowers have parts in fives and two bracts on their stalks.

Sweet violet

Viola odorata

Fl 1.5 cm

Lvs round to 6 cm

Down-pointed hrs on lf stk; fls frag, spls blunt. *Ht:* 10 cm; *D:* T (not far N); *Fl:* 2–4

Common dog violet

V. riviniana

Fl 2 cm pale spur

Near-hrlss, rosette of lvs; appendages on spls, spur notched. *Ht:* 15 cm; *D:* T; *Fl:* 4–6

Early dog violet

V. reichenbachiana

Spur dark purple

No hrs on fl shs, spl appendages small, spur unnotched. *Ht:* 15 cm; *D:* W, C; *Fl:* 3–5

Hairy violet

V. hirta

Hrs on lf stk spread

Not frag. Lvs hry, more pointed than *V. odorata*, spls round. *Ht:* 20 cm; *D:* T; *Fl:* 4

Teesdale violet

V. rupestris

Many short hrs, central lf rosette, lvs round, hry stks, fr hry. *Ht:* 3 cm; *D:* T; *Fl:* 5

Bog violet

V. persicifolia

Fl to 1.5 cm, rounded

Erect, lf blade longer than stk. Fls purple-veined, spur green. *Ht:* 15 cm; *D:* T; *Fl:* 5–6

Marsh violet

V. palustris

Lvs kidney-shaped

No uprt stems, lf blade to 4 cm. Fl 1 cm, ptls pale, dark veins, spls blunt. *D:* T; *Fl:* 4–7

Heath violet

V. canina

Spur on fl yellow-green

Creeping per, no lf rosette. Lvs not as notched at base as other spp. *Ht:* 20 cm; *D:* T; *Fl:* 4–6

Wild pansy

V. tricolor

Ptls longer than spls

Fl stks long, to 8 cm

Stipules lobed, centre lobe not indented; spur longer than spl appendages. *Ht:* 30 cm; *D:* T; *Fl:* 4–9

Field pansy

V. arvensis

Ptls shorter than spls

Centre stipule lobe indented. Spur equals spl appendages, fl less than 2 cm. *Ht:* 30 cm; *D:* T; *Fl:* 4–10

Rockrose family Cistaceae

Shrubs or herbs with opposite, hairy, unlobed leaves. Flowers have 3 or 5 sepals, 5 petals and many stamens.

Common rockrose

Helianthemum nummularium

Fl to 3 cm

Straggles to 30 cm. Lvs stipuled, woolly below. Infl loose, style not bent. *D:* T (not far N); *Fl:* 6–9

White rockrose

H. apenninum

Spls hry

Like *H. nummularium* except in fl col. Lvs woolly all over, curled edges. *Ht:* 25 cm; *D:* SW; *Fl:* 5–7

Hoary rockrose

H. canum

Fl to 1.5 cm

Leaves small, oval, no stipules, small fl, bent style. *Ht:* 10 cm; *D:* C, S; *Fl:* 5–7

Spotted rockrose

Tuberaria guttata

Ptls have spot

Erect, hry lvs unstkd, stipuled, terminal infl, no styles. *Ht:* 20 cm; *D:* S, W; *Fl:* 5–8

Common fumana

Fumana procumbens

Prostrate, brs 30 cm; lvs alt, no stipules; fls sol, stks as long as lvs. *D:* S, W; *Fl:* 5

Water chestnut family Trapaceae

Annual aquatics with large woody fruits. Leaves in a rosette have inflated stalks. Flower parts are in fours.

Water chestnut

Trapa natans   **Floating lf blades** *to 4 cm*

Pointed spls *form horns on woody fr*

Robust submerged stems unbranched to 2 m. Lf stks to 17 cm, hry, swollen. Fls in lf axils, ptls 8 mm. Locally cultivated. *D:* S, C; *Fl:* 6–7

Willowherb family Onagraceae

Annuals or perennials. Single or terminally grouped flowers usually have 4 unjoined petals and sepals and 8 stamens.

Rosebay willowherb

Epilobium angustifolium

Fl *to 3 cm*

Lvs narrow
Erect, lfy per. Lvs spiral, serrate; 2 top ptls larger than lower 2, stamens and style protrude; fr 7 cm. *Ht:* 1 m; *D:* T; *Fl:* 7–9

Broad-leaved willowherb

E. montanum

Fl *to 9 mm*

Lvs opp, short-stkd

Shs uprt

Broad lvs rounded at base. Ptls notched, stigma 4-lobed. *Ht:* 40 cm; *D:* T; *Fl:* 6–8

Alpine willowherb

E. anagallidifolium

Fl *to 5 mm*

Lvs to 2 cm

Stems prostrate, 2 faint ridges, erect fl shs to 10 cm. Lvs in prs. *D:* T (not far N); *Fl:* 7–8

Marsh willowherb

E. palustre

Stem *has no raised lines*

Lvs unstkd

Fine stolons, bulbous at tips. Fl 5 mm, stigma unlobed. *Ht:* 40 cm; *D:* T; *Fl:* 7–8

Great willowherb

E. hirsutum

Fl 2 cm

Very hry; stigma 4–lobed, longer than stms. *Ht:* 1.2 m; *D:* T (not far N); *Fl:* 7–8

Large-flowered evening primrose

Oenothera erythrosepala

Robust, stem hry to 1 m, lvs spiral, buds big, ridged, spls red striped, 4 ptls to 5 cm. *D:* W, C; *Fl:* 6–9

Hoary willowherb

E. parviflorum

Fl under 1 cm

Plant softly hry

Leaves do not run into stem; 4-lobed stigma equals stms. *Ht:* 80 cm; *D:* T (not N); *Fl:* 7–8

Enchanter's nightshade

Circaea lutetiana

Has stolons and few hrs; 2 deep-notched ptls and spls. *Ht:* 50 cm; *D:* T; *Fl:* 6–8

Hampshire purslane

Ludwigia palustris

Lvs to 2 cm in opp prs

Fl 3 mm

Aquatic, shs slender to 30 cm. Fls sol in axils, 4 spread spls, no ptls. *D:* W, C, S; *Fl:* 6

American willowherb

E. adenocaulon

Fl to 6 mm

Lvs to 10 cm

Stem hry, 4 raised lines; lvs short-stalked; stigma unlobed. *Ht:* 80 cm; *D:* NW; *Fl:* 6–8

Alpine enchanter's nightshade

C. alpina

Fr hooked

Lvs opp, stkd

Has tuberous stock, fl shs space out in fr, ptls notched. *Ht:* 20 cm; *D:* N; *Fl:* 7–8

Sea heath family Frankeniaceae

Dwarf shrubs with opposite leaves. Flowers have 4–6 sepals and petals and 6 stamens. The fruit is a capsule.

Sea heath

Frankenia laevis

Fl *5 mm, 5 ptls and spls, 6 stamens*

Delicate mat-forming, prostrate woody per resembling spp of *Erica* (p 93). Lvs densely crowded. *Ht:* to 15 cm; *D:* W; *Fl:* 7–8

Cucumber family Cucurbitaceae

Mostly succulent, tendrilled, hairy annual climbers. Flowers have parts in fives and petals often joined at the base.

White bryony

Bryonia cretica

Stems *bristly, angled, branched near base*

Fl *to 2 cm*

Fr *a red berry*

Scrambles to 3 m. Tendrils arise from stem near lvs. ♂, ♀ fls on separate plants, veined ptls longer than spls, 3 stigmas 2 × cut. *D:* S, W; *Fl:* 5–9

Loosestrife family Lythraceae

Herbs or shrubs with whorled leaves without stipules. The petals are joined to the sepals which are united in a tube.

Purple loosestrife   Grass poly

Lythrum salicaria

Fl *to 1.5 cm*

Infl *a spike to 30 cm*

L. hyssopifolia

Lvs *unstkd to 1.5 cm*

Stem 4-angled; lvs unstkd, opp or in whorls of 3. Fls have 4–6 ptls. *Ht:* 1 m; *D:* T (not far N); *Fl:* 6–8

Much branched,hrlss. Fls 5 mm, sol in lf axils, 6 stamens. *Ht:* 15 cm; *D:* S, W, C; *Fl:* 6–7

Water milfoil family Haloragaceae
Marestail family Hippuridaceae

Aquatics often with whorled leaves. Solitary marestail flowers hve no sepals or petals and one stamen. Water milfoil flowers have tiny petals and sepals and 8 stamens.

Spiked water milfoil

Myriophyllum spicatum **Fls in whorls of 4**

Branched submerged shs to 2.5 m. Lvs 4 per whorl, 13–35 narrow lobes, fl bracts entire. *D:* T; *Fl:* 6–7

Whorled water milfoil

M. verticillatum **Lvs 25–35 lobes, 5 per whorl**

Submerged shs to 3 m. Fl spike to 25 cm above water, fls in whorls of 5, bracts pinnate. *D:* T; *Fl:* 7–8

Alternate-leaved water milfoil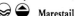

M. alterniflorum **Lvs to 2.5 cm, 6–18 lobes, in whorls of 4**

Stems *branched, slender*
Submerged shs to 1.2 m. Fl spike droops in bud, fls in whorls, ♀ at base, ♂ above, bracts pinnate below, simple above. *D:* W, C, N; *Fl:* 5–8

Marestail

Hippuris vulgaris

Emergent, with rhizome. Lvs unlobed in whorls of 6–12. *Ht:* 60 cm; *D:* T; *Fl:* 6–7

Dogwood family Cornaceae

Mostly trees and shrubs rather than herbs. Flowers have parts in fours (the sepals are small) above the ovary.

Dwarf cornel

Cornus suecica

Fr *5 mm*

Perennial, shs erect. Lvs in opp prs, parallel veins. Infl an umbel of 8–25 fls to 2 mm with 4 bracts to 8 mm. *Ht:* 15 cm; *D:* N; *Fl:* 7–8

Ivy family Araliaceae

Evergreen woody climbers. Flowers in umbels have sepals joined in a 5-toothed tube and 5 petals and stamens.

Ivy

Hedera helix

Ptls to 4 mm

Fr to 8 mm

Climbs to 30 m, using rts on trees. Lvs hrlss, 3–5 lobes; infl gps of umbels on climbing shs only, fr berry-like. *D:* W, C, S; *Fl:* 9–11

Carrot family Umbelliferae

Herbs, often with hollow, furrowed stems. Leaves have sheathing stalks. Flowers in groups of umbels with bracts and/or bracteoles have parts in fives and sepals united in a tube.

Hogweed

Heracleum sphondylium

Lvs to 60 cm

Fls to 1 cm

Fr to 8 mm

Umbel to 15 cm diam

Bristly, stems hollow; lvs 1-pinnate. Bracteoles but no bracts in infl, outer fls have unequal ptls. *Ht:* 1.5 m; *D:* T (not far N); *Fl:* 6–9

Upright hedge parsley

Torilis japonica

Fr 4 mm

Umbel 5–15 rays, 4–6 bracts, hooked spines on fr. *Ht:* 1 m; *D:* T (not far N); *Fl:* 7–8

Knotted bur parsley

T. nodosa

Stems solid

Fr to 3 mm

Short-stkd umbel, no bracts, long bracteoles. Fr spines straight. *Ht:* 20 cm; *D:* S, W; *Fl:* 5–7

Spreading bur parsley

T. arvensis

Fr to 5 mm

Stems solid

Umbel 3–5 rays, 1 or no bracts, spines on fr curved. *Ht:* 25 cm; *D:* W, S, C; *Fl:* 7–9

Cow parsley

Anthriscus sylvestris

Umbel 4–10 rays, no hrs or bracts; fr to 5 mm, smooth. *Ht:* 80 cm; *D:* T; *Fl:* 4–6

Bur chervil

A. caucalis

Umbel has bracteoles, no bracts; spines on fr hooked. *Ht:* 35 cm; *D:* W, C, S; *Fl:* 5–6

Stems *hrlss all over*

Fr 3 mm

Greater bur parsley

Turgenia latifolia

Umbel *long-stkd, 2–5 rays*

Fr to 1 cm

Leaves 1-pinnate, hry below; fr has rows of spines. *Ht:* 45 cm; *D:* S, C; *Fl:* 5–8

Small bur parsley

Caucalis platycarpos

Lvs *hrlss*

Sepal tube has obvious teeth; fr has spineless ridges. *Ht:* 20 cm; *D:* T (not far N); *Fl:* 6–7

Stone parsley

Sison amomum

Fetid smell, hrlss; umbel 3–6 rayed, fr round. *Ht:* 80 cm; *D:* S, W; *Fl:* 7–9

Cambridge milk parsley

Selinum carvifolia

Stems solid, hrlss, winged ridges, no spl teeth; fr 4 mm. *Ht:* 80 cm; *D:* T; *Fl:* 7–10

Rough chervil

Chaerophyllum temulentum

Stems bristly, spotted; bracts reflexed in fr; fr tapered. *Ht:* 80 cm; *D:* T (not N); *Fl:* 6–7

Hemlock

Conium maculatum

Stems spotted; infl 10–20 rays, fr 3 mm, wavy ridges. *Ht:* 2 m; *D:* T (not N); *Fl:* 6–7

Coriander

Coriandrum sativum

Umbel *3–5 rays*

Leaves 1–2 pinnate; ptls vary in size, frs stick in groups. *Ht:* 55 cm; *D:* S; *Fl:* 6

Pignut

Conopodium majus

Hairless, hollow stem. Umbels to 7 cm, 6–12 rays. Fr 4 mm has prominent uprt styles; tubers edible. *Ht:* 40 cm; *D:* W; *Fl:* 5–6

Great pignut

Bunium bulbocastanum

Stem solid. Fr to 3 mm has curved, short styles. *Ht:* 50 cm; *D: S, C;* Fl: *6–7*

Fool's parsley

Aethusa cynapium

Umbel 10–20 rays, 3–4 bracteoles on outer part, no bracts; fr to 4 mm. *Ht:* 1 m; *D:* T; *Fl:* 7–8

Wild carrot

Daucus carota

Infl to 7 cm diam

Bristly, stem solid, many rays in infl, bracts lobed; fr ridged, spiny. *Ht:* 80 cm; *D:* T; *Fl:* 6–8

Moon carrot

Seseli libanotis

Stems have fibrous base. Umbels long-stkd to 6 cm diam, many bracts and bracteoles. *Ht:* 45 cm; *D:* T (not far N); *Fl:* 7–8

Caraway

Carum carvi

Lvs fine-lobed

Leaves 2-pinnate. No bracts or bracteoles; fr strong smelling. *Ht:* 40 cm; *D:* T; *Fl:* 6–7

Whorled caraway

C. verticillatum

Leaves 1-pinnate, look whorled. Some bracts and bracteoles. *Ht:* 45 cm; *D:* W; *Fl:* 7–8

Honewort

Trinia glauca

Plant glaucous

Male umbels 1 cm, ♀ 3 cm on separate plants. *Ht:* 15 cm; *D:* W, C, S; *Fl:* 5–6

Greater water parsnip

Sium latifolium

Leaves 1-pinnate, 4–6 lflt prs, serrate; infl 20+ rays; fr oval. *Ht:* 1.5 m; *D:* T; *Fl:* 7–8

Fr 3 mm

Lesser water parsnip

Berula erecta

Lflts *serrate*

Leaves 1-pinnate, 7–10 lflt prs; infl 10–20 rays. *Ht:* to 1 m; *D:* T (not far N); *Fl:* 7–9

Spignel

Meum anthamaticum

Aromatic, lf segments fine; umbel 6–15 rays; fr to 1 cm. *Ht:* 45 cm; *D:* W, C; *Fl:* 6–7

Angelica

Angelica sylvestris

Stems have bloom (unlike *A. archangelica*); lvs 2–3 pinnate, stks inflated. *Ht:* 1.5 m; *D:* T; *Fl:* 7–9

Cowbane

Cicuta virosa

Plant *v poisonous*

Leaflets narrow, serrate. Many bracteoles longer than fl stks. *Ht:* to 1.3 m; *D:* T; *Fl:* 7–8

Sermountain

Laserpitium latifolium

Lflts *hry below*

Umbel has many bracts, few bracteoles. Fr to 1 cm has wavy wings. *Ht:* 1.2 m; *D:* T (not UK); *Fl:* 6–8

Sweet cicely

Myrrhis odorata

Strongly aromatic. Some fls ♂ only. Fr to 2.5 cm. *Ht:* to 1 m; *D:* W, mts in S; *Fl:* 5–6

Corn parsley

Petroselinum segetum

Lower brs spreading; lvs 1-pinnate, umbels irregular. *Ht:* to 1 m; *D:* W; *Fl:* 8–9

Milk parsley

Peucedanum palustre

Umbel has 4 bracts bent back, long thin bracteoles. *Ht:* to 1.5 m; *D:* T; *Fl:* 7–9

Hog's fennel

P. officinale

Linear, tangled lflts; infl 20+ rays, often no bracteoles. *Ht:* 1 m; *D:* S, C; *Fl:* 7–9

Field eryngo

Eryngium campestre

Basal lvs pinnate, stkd. Bracts spiny, bracteoles 2–3 × fl length. *Ht:* 45 cm; *D:* C, S; *Fl:* 7–8

Sea holly

E. maritimum

Fl 8 mm

Glaucous. Bracts spiny, toothed, bracteoles just longer than fls. *Ht:* 45 cm; *D:* T; *Fl:* 7–8

Rock samphire

Crithmum maritimum

Fleshy per to 30 cm. Lf segs cylindrical; many bracts and bracteoles in umbel. Fr to 6 mm, egg-shaped. *D:* T (not N); *Fl:* 6–8

Burnet saxifrage

Pimpinella saxifraga

Stems flexible

Basal lvs 1-pinnate, stem lvs 2-pinnate; no bracts or bracteoles. *Ht:* 1 m; *D:* T; *Fl:* 7–8

Greater burnet saxifrage

P. major

Stems rigid, brittle; lvs 1-pinnate; no bracts or bracteoles. *Ht:* 1 m; *D:* T; *Fl:* 6–7

Ground elder

Aegopodium podagraria
Umbel *to 6 cm diam*

Fr 4 mm

Creeps to 1 m. Lf segments *c.* 5 cm long, serrate.
No bracts or bracteoles. *D:* T; *Fl:* 5–7

Shepherd's needle

*Scandix
pecten-veneris*

Umbels 2–3 rays;
bracteoles lobed, 1 cm;
fr ridged. *Ht:* 35 cm;
D: W, C, S; *Fl:* 4–7

Hemlock water dropwort

Oenanthe crocata

Has rt tubers; lvs 3–4
pinnate to 50 cm; v
poisonous. *Ht:* 1.2 m;
D: W; *Fl:* 6–7

Parsley water dropwort

O. lachenalii

*L flts
linear*

Pinnate part of lf longer
than solid stk. Fr 2 mm,
stk swollen. *Ht:* 1 m;
D: W; *Fl:* 6–9

Water dropwort

O. fistulosa

Pinnate part of lf
shorter than hollow
stk. *Ht:* 45 cm; *D:* W,
C, S; *Fl:* 7–9

Fine-leaved water dropwort

O. aquatica

Umbel
short-stkd

*Lvs
3-pinnate*

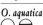

Roots fibrous; lower
lvs submerged; umbels
opp lvs. *Ht:* 1.2 m; *D:*
T (not far N); *Fl:* 6–9

Wild celery

Apium graveolens

Top stem lvs 3-lobed,
no bracts or bracteoles;
celery smell. *Ht:* 40 cm;
D: T; *Fl:* 6–8

Fool's watercress

A. nodiflorum

Often prostrate to 1 m;
umbels unstkd, no
bracts, 5 bracteoles. *D:*
T; *Fl:* 7–8

89

Sickle hare's ear

Bupleurum falcatum

Hollow-stemmed per; bracteoles shorter than fls. *Ht:* to 1.3 m; *D:* S, C, E; *Fl:* 7–10

Smallest hare's ear

B. tenuissimum

Plant *annual*

Umbels to 5 mm in lf axils; fls shorter than bracteoles. *Ht:* 35 cm; *D:* S, W, C; *Fl:* 7–9

Thorow-wax

B. rotundifolium

Plant *annual*

Glaucous, lvs round, encircling stem, oval bracteoles. *Ht:* 20 cm; *D:* C, S; *Fl:* 6–7

Scots lovage

Ligusticum scoticum

Fr 4 mm, ridged

Hairless per to 90 cm. Upper lvs 3-lobed, serrate, basal lvs 2-pinnate. *D:* N; *Fl:* 7

Fennel

Foeniculum vulgare

Glaucous, strong smell. Lvs cut into v fine segs. *Ht:* 1 m; *D:* T (not N); *Fl:* 7–10

Alexanders

Smyrnium olusatrum

Lf stks *sheathing, inflated*

Leaves pinnate, shiny with 3-lobed segs; fr 8 mm, black. *Ht:* to 1.5 m; *D:* S; *Fl:* 4–6

Marsh pennywort

Hydrocotyle vulgaris

Umbel *2–7 fls*

Creeping per. Lvs circular to 5 cm diam on long erect stks to 25 cm. *D:* W, C, S; *Fl:* 7–10

Pepper saxifrage
Silaum silaus

Hairless per; lvs 2–3 pinnate, fine-toothed segs. *Ht:* to 1 m; *D:* W, C, E; *Fl:* 6–8

Astrantia
Astrantia major

Bracts *linear to 2 cm, whitish below*

Has creeping stock. Basal lvs to 15 cm, palmate; some fls ♂ only. *Ht:* 60 cm; *D:* C; *Fl:* 5–7

Sanicle
Sanicula europaea

Hairless per to 60 cm; basal lvs round to 6 cm, 3–5 lobes; fr 3 mm. *D:* T; *Fl:* 5–9

Wild parsnip
Pastinaca sativa

Leaves 1-pinnate, shs hollow; fr to 8 mm, pointed. *Ht:* 1.2 m; *D:* T (not far N); *Fl:* 7–8

Bladderseed
Physospermum cornubiense

Leaves and umbels long-stkd; fr 5 mm, styles bent back. *Ht:* 55 cm; *D:* S; *Fl:* 7–8

Diapensia family Diapensiaceae

Arctic perennials and dwarf shrubs. Sepals and petals are in a 5-lobed tube, the stigma is three-lobed.

Diapensia

Diapensia lapponica

Ptls *1 cm*

Lvs *to 1 cm*

Woody, cushion-forming per to 5 cm. Lvs unlobed, narrowing to short stk. Fls sol, fl stks to 3 cm. Spl tube 5 mm. *D:* N; *Fl:* 5–6

Wintergreen family Pyrolaceae

Perennial evergreen herbs with rhizomes. The symmetrical flowers have parts in fives and the petals are not united in a tube. The 5-celled ovary has a single stigma.

Common wintergreen

Pyrola minor　　　*Fl 6 mm*

Creeping; lvs alt, short-stkd. Fls spherical, style straight, stigma 5-lobed. *Ht:* 20 cm; *D:* T; *Fl:* 6–8

Round-leaved wintergreen

P. rotundifolia　　*Fl 1.2 cm*

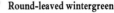

Leaves alt, stk longer than blade. Long, curved style makes ring under stigma. *Ht:* 25 cm; *D:* T; *Fl:* 7–9

Yellow wintergreen

P. chlorantha

Like *P. rotundifolia* but lvs pale above, obovate; fls yellow-green. *Ht:* 20 cm; *D:* T (not W); *Fl:* 7–9

Umbellate wintergreen

Chimaphila umbellata

Leaves serrate, appear whorled; fls in an umbel, v short styles, ptls spread. *Ht:* 20 cm; *D:* N, C, E; *Fl:* 6–7

One-flowered wintergreen

Moneses uniflora

Fl 1.5 cm

Leaves opp, rounded, short-stkd. Fl shs to 15 cm, fls sol wide open. *D:* T; *Fl:* 6–8

Toothed wintergreen

Orthilia secunda

Leaves serrate; fl shs 10 cm, fls all to one side, stigmas projecting. *D:* T; *Fl:* 7–8

Yellow birdsnest

Monotropa hypopitys

Fl hry inside

Has no green parts. Waxy stems to 30 cm, fls drooping, fr erect. *D:* T; *Fl:* 6–8

Heather family Ericaceae

Dwarf shrubs with simple evergreen leaves. The flowers, usually in clusters, have petals fused into a tube to which the stamens are not attached and a single style.

Cross-leaved heath

Erica tetralix

Ptls *v pale*

Leaves hry in whorls of 4; infl terminal, dense, spls hry. *Ht:* 50 cm; *D:* W, N; *Fl:* 7–9

Heather

Calluna vulgaris

Fls *not clustered*

Tightly inrolled lvs overlapping, may be hry; 4 bracteoles at base of each fl. *Ht:* 60 cm; *D:* T; *Fl:* 7–9

Bell heather

E. cinerea

Spls *hrlss*

Leaves hrlss in whorls of 3; infl less dense than *E. tetralix*. *Ht:* 55 cm; *D:* W; *Fl:* 7–9

Dorset heath

E. ciliaris

Stems *have short hrs*

Erect to 80 cm, lvs in whorls of 3, hry at edges, infl one-sided. *D:* W; *Fl:* 6–9

Cornish heath

E. vagans

Ptl tube *wide, stamens protruding*

Hairless; lvs in whorls of 4–5. Infl dense, each fl on long stk. *Ht:* 60 cm; *D:* W; *Fl:* 7–8

Spring heather

E. herbacea

Plant *prostrate*

Leaves in whorls of 4, stamens project from ptl tube. *Ht:* 15 cm; *D:* S, C; *Fl:* 12–3

Irish heath

E. erigena

Plant *hrlss*

Leaves in whorls of 4; fls not inflated, stamens just project. *Ht:* to 2 m; *D:* SW; *Fl:* 3–5

St Dabeoc's heath

Daboecia cantabrica

Lvs *to 1 cm*

Stems hry, lvs white below. Infl 3–10 fls, 4 hry spls. *Ht:* 35 cm; *D:* W; *Fl:* 7–9

Bilberry

Vaccinium myrtillus

Lvs *serrate*

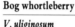

Fr *8 mm*

Deciduous, stems green, v ridged; berry black with bloom. *Ht:* 45 cm; *D:* T; *Fl:* 4–6

Cowberry

V. vitis-idaea

Lvs *dull below*

Evergreen, lvs round, glossy above; fl 6 mm, bell shaped. *Ht:* 20 cm; *D:* N, C; *Fl:* 6–8

Cranberry

V. oxycoccos

Creeps to 80 cm, shs slender, lvs oval. Ptl tube cut almost to base *D:* N, C; *Fl:* 6–8

Bog whortleberry

V. uliginosum

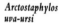

Stems round, lvs untoothed, decid; fr has bloom. *Ht:* 40 cm; *D:* N, C; *Fl:* 5–6

Alpine bearberry

Arctostaphylos uva-ursi

Lvs *blunt*

Prostrate evergreen to 2 m. Infl 5–12 fls, fr to 8 mm, red, tastes dry. *D:* T; *Fl:* 5–7

Black bearberry

A. alpinus

Prostrate, decid to 2 m; serrate lvs strongly veined; fr juicy, black to 1 cm. *D:* S mts, N; *Fl:* 5–8

Wild azalea

Loiseleuria procumbens

Fl *has 5 stamens*

Prostrate, evergreen to 30 cm, lvs numerous, opp to 8 mm; ptls have spreading lobes. *D:* T; *Fl:* 5–7

Mountain heather

Phyllodoce caerulea

Erect evergreen; lvs dense, fls to 8 mm, long-stkd, 5 stamens in terminal infl. *Ht:* 10 cm; *D:* N; *Fl:* 6–7

Leatherleaf

Chamaedaphne calyculata

Fl to 6 mm

Erect evergreen, lvs slightly serrate, scaly below to 4 cm; infl 5–20 drooping fls. *Ht:* 35 cm; *D:* NE; *Fl:* 6–7

Bog rosemary

Andromeda polifolia

Fl 6 mm

Creeping evergreen to 30 cm. Lvs elongate to 3.5 cm, darker above; fls long-stkd, infl 2–8 fls. *D:* T; *Fl:* 5–6

Ledum

Ledum palustre

Lvs to 4.5 cm

Many rust coloured hrs on stems and lf undersides; fls long-stkd, infl dense. *Ht:* 80 cm; *D:* N, C; *Fl:* 6–7

Rhododendron

Rhododendron ponticum

Evergreen to 3 m; lvs hrlss, paler below. Infl dense, fls open, bell shaped, 10 stamens. *D:* W; *Fl:* 5–6

Crowberry family Empetraceae

Heath-like dwarf evergreens with 6 sepal and petal lobes that are not brightly coloured and three stamens.

Crowberry

Empetrum nigrum

Fl to 2 mm diam Fr 5 mm

Prostrate evergreen to 30 cm, stems red. Lvs linear, white line below; fls in lf axils in gps of 1–3; fr round, black. *D:* S mts, N; *Fl:* 5–6

Primrose family Primulaceae

Simple-leaved herbs. Symmetrical tubular flowers have parts in fives and stamens joined to the petal tube interior.

Primrose

Primula vulgaris

Fl 3 cm

Lvs to 15 cm

Leaves hrlss above thin gradually to base; indiv fl shs to 10 cm have long hrs. *D*: W, S; *Fl*: 12–5

Cowslip

P. veris

Fl to 1.5 cm

Infl 1–30 fls

Lvs to 15 cm

Hairy lvs narrow sharply; orange-spotted fls on common 20 cm sh (scape). *D*: T (not far N); *Fl*: 4–5

Birdseye primrose

P. farinosa

Ptl lobes spread

Lvs mealy below

White lvs have crinkly edges; fr longer than spl tube, scape 10 cm. *D*: mts T; *Fl*: 5–6

Scottish primrose

P. scotica

Fl 6 mm, ptl lobes closed

As *P. farinosa* but lvs uncrinkled, fr almost equals spl tube, scape 6 cm. *D*: Scot; *Fl*: 5–9

Scandinavian primrose

P. scandinavica

Like *P. scotica* but scape to 10 cm, fl to 1 cm, longer bracts. *D*: Scand mts; *Fl*: 6–9

Oxlip

P. elatior

Fl to 1.8 cm

Lvs to 20 cm

Leaves as *P. veris* but hrs curled; scape to 30 cm, hry; spl tube has dark ridges. *D*: S, W, C; *Fl*: 4–5

Auricula

P. auricula

Broad lvs hrlss, succ, thick at edges; scape to 16 cm, infl to 30 fls. *D*: Alps, Carp; *Fl*: 5–7

Cyclamen

Cyclamen purpurascens

Fl to 3 cm

Lf to 8 cm

Tuberous base to 3 cm, lf edges rounded, ptl lobes clawless below, fl sh to 15 cm. *D:* C, S; *Fl:* 6–10

Chickweed wintergreen

Trientalis europaea

Fl to 1.8 cm

Lvs rigid, pointed, unstkd

Erect, hrlss stems to 25 cm not branched; 1 or 2 fls on stks to 7 cm from lf whorl. *D:* S mts, N; *Fl:* 6–7

Scarlet pimpernel

Anagallis arvensis

Prostrate, stems square; lvs opp, spots below; fl stks slim, globular fr. *Ht:* 20 cm; *D:* T; *Fl:* 6–8

Sowbread

C. hederifolium

Corm to 15 cm; lvs to 14 cm, angled edges. Ptl lobes to 2 cm, clawed at base; fl sh to 30 cm, coiled fr stk. *D:* S; *Fl:* 8–11

Large androsace

Androsace maxima

Fl 6 mm

Lvs 3 cm

Annual; 1 to sev 8 cm scapes, bracts large, lfy; spls longer than ptls. *D:* S, C; *Fl:* 4–5

Alpine snowbell

Soldanella alpina

Round, long-stkd lvs to 4 cm wide. Fl to 1.3 cm, many narrow lobes, fl sh to 15 cm. *D:* S, C; *Fl:* 4–7

White androsace

A. lactea

Fl stks long

Tufted per; lvs linear sessile; sev scapes to 15 cm. Stolons present. *D:* S, C; *Fl:* 6–8

Bog pimpernel

A. tenella

Fl 1 cm

Stems round; lvs opp, shorter than slim fl shs. Ptl tube longer than spls. *Ht:* 10 cm; *D:* W; *Fl:* 6–8

Yellow loosestrife

Lysimachia vulgaris

Lvs *dotted*

Rhizomatous per; lvs in whorls of 2–4; fl shs slim, fl 1.5 cm. *Ht:* 1 m; *D:* T; *Fl:* 7–8

Tufted loosestrife

L. thyrsiflora

Stamens *just protrude*

Rhizomatous per, lvs in opp prs, dotted black. Infl dense in lf axils. *Ht:* 45 cm; *D:* T (not S); *Fl:* 6–7

Sea milkwort

Glaux maritima

Creeping succ, opp lvs in 4 ranks; unstkd fls in lf axils, no ptls, 5 ptl-like spls. *Ht:* 20 cm; *D:* T; *Fl:* 6–8

Water violet

Hottonia palustris

Fl *to 2.5 cm*

Lf lobes *linear*

Floating, hrlss; lvs pinnate in whorls; fl scape 30 cm erect. *D:* T (not far N); *Fl:* 5–6

Yellow pimpernel

L. nemorum

Fl *1.2 cm, fl sh long, slim*

Lvs *dotted, oval*

Slender prostrate per; lvs opp, short-stkd. Fls sol, fr globular. *Ht:* 30 cm; *D:* W, C; *Fl:* 5–9

Creeping Jenny

L. nummularia

Fls *sol*

Lvs *opp, round, dotted*

Prostrate stems to 60 cm little branched. Fl shs robust, shorter than lvs. *D:* T; *Fl:* 6–8

Brookweed

Samolus valerandi

Fl stk *to 1.5 cm*

Stems lfy, no brs, lvs alt; fl stks slim in lf axils. *Ht:* 35 cm; *D:* W, C; *Fl:* 6–8

Sea lavender family Plumbaginaceae

Simple-leaved perennials. Clustered flowers have parts in fives—sepals in a tube and petals just joined below.

Thrift

Armeria maritima

Fl head dense

Dense basal lf rosette, lvs narrow, 1-veined. Scape to 30 cm, short-stkd 8 mm fls, lobes of spl tube sharply pointed. *D:* T; *Fl:* 4–10

Jersey thrift

A. alliacea

Lvs broad

As *A. maritima* but scape to 60 cm; lvs 3–5 veined; points on spl tube long, hr-like. *D:* SW; *Fl:* 6–9

Sea lavender

Limonium vulgare

Lvs to 12 cm

Leaves succ, veins pinnate; scape to 30 cm, many fls on short stks, infl branched. *D:* S; *Fl:* 7–10

Rock sea lavender

L. binervosum

Like *L. vulgare* but lvs smaller, rounder, no pinnate veins, 3 veins below. *Ht:* 20 cm; *D:* W; *Fl:* 7–9

Gentian family Gentianaceae

Hairless herbs with simple stalkless opposite leaves and tubular 4–5 lobed flowers. The stamens join the petals.

Marsh gentian

Gentiana pneumonanthe

Fl to 4 cm   **Lvs** linear to 4 cm

Erect per to 40 cm. Terminal infl 1–7 fls, spl lobes joined by membrane as in all *Gentiana* spp, ptl lobes 3-veined. *D:* T (not far N); *Fl:* 8–9

Spring gentian

Gentiana verna

Ptl tube
2 cm long

Perennial; lvs to 1.5 cm in rosettes make a compact cushion. Fls sol, terminal, spl tube ridged. *Ht:* 4 cm; *D:* C; *Fl:* 4–6

Great yellow gentian

G. lutea

Robust, uprt per to 1.2 m. Fls crowded in lf axils and at apex, ptl tube has 5–9 lobes longer than tube. *D:* C, S mts; *Fl:* 6–8

Alpine gentian

G. nivalis

Lvs
to 5 mm

Delicate uprt ann; fls sol, ptl tube to 1.5 cm. *Ht:* to 15 cm; *D:* N, S; *Fl:* 7–9

Purple gentian

G. purpurea   *Spl tube split*

Stem lvs
unstkd

Erect per to 30 cm. Fls clustered at apex and in lf axils, ptls spotted. *D:* C; *Fl:* 7–8

Slender gentian

Gentianella tenella

Flowers much shorter than fl shs, spl tube deeply cut. *Ht:* 7 cm; *D:* T (not UK); *Fl:* 7–8

Cross gentian

G. cruciata

Flowers in terminal gps, ptl tube 2 cm, 4-lobed. *Ht:* 35 cm; *D:* S, C, E; *Fl:* 6–9

Stem lvs
many,
unstkd

Autumn gentian

Gentianella amarella

Fls
unstkd

Sepal tube cut to under ¾ of length, 4 or 5 equal spl lobes. *Ht:* 20 cm; *D:* N, C; *Fl:* 7–10

Field gentian

Gentianella campestris

Flower parts in 4s, 2 outer lobes of spl tube much longer than other 2. *Ht:* 20 cm; *D:* N, C; *Fl:* 7–10

Fringed gentian

G. ciliata

Ptls 2× spl tube

Flowers sol or in loose clusters, 4 ptl lobes, fringed at edges. *Ht:* 17 cm; *D:* T (not N, W); *Fl:* 8–10

Northern gentian

G. aurea

Ptl lobes to 1 cm diam

Flowers in dense terminal gps, 4 or 5 ptl lobes. *Ht:* 10 cm; *D:* Arct; *Fl:* 7–8

Common centaury

Centaurium erythraea

Fls unstkd   **Plant** erect

Rounded oval lvs to 5 cm long, 2 cm diam in basal rosette. *Ht:* 30 cm; *D:* T (not far N); *Fl:* 6–10

Seaside centaury

C. littorale   **Infl** dense

Leaves in basal rosette 2 cm long, under 5 mm diam, fls unstkd. *Ht:* 15 cm; *D:* NW, EC; *Fl:* 7–8

Yellow wort

Blackstonia perfoliata

Glaucous ann; fls to 1.5 cm, 6–8 ptl and spl lobes. *Ht:* 30 cm; *D:* W, C, S; *Fl:* 6–10

Marsh felwort

Swertia perennis

Fl c. 3 cm diam

Petal and spl tubes 4–5 lobed, cut nearly to base. *Ht:* 45 cm; *D:* mts T (not UK); *Fl:* 7–9

Yellow centaury

Cicendia filiformis

Delicate ann, long-stkd fls to 5 mm, 4 ptl lobes. Lvs to 6 mm. *Ht:* 8 cm; *D:* W, S; *Fl:* 6–10

Bogbean family Menyanthaceae

Alternate-leaved aquatics. The 5 petals and sepals are in deep-lobed tubes; the stamens join the petal tube.

Bogbean

Menyanthes trifoliata

Fl stks c. 1 cm

Fringed water lily

Nymphoides peltata

Fl stks to 7 cm

Flower stks and 3-lobed lvs above water. Ptl tube 1.5 cm, fringed edges. *Ht:* 20 cm; *D:* T; *Fl:* 5–7

Leaves 8 cm, v notched at base. Fls 3 cm, long-stkd, fringed ptl lobes. *D:* T (not far N); *Fl:* 7–8

Periwinkle family Apocynaceae

Woody plants with symmetrical 5-part flowers. The petal lobes twist in bud and the stamens join the petal tube.

Lesser periwinkle

Vinca minor

Greater periwinkle

V. major

Creeps to 60 cm. Lvs v short-stkd, hrlss; fls sol to 3 cm, spl tube hrlss. *D:* S, W, C; *Fl:* 3–5

Scrambles to 1 m. Lf stks to 1 cm, fl shs uprt, fls to 5 cm, spl lobes hry at edge. *D:* W, C; *Fl:* 4–6

Milkweed family Asclepiadaceae

Perennials often with milky sap. Tubular flowers have parts in fives; stamens fused in a ring join the stigma.

Vincetoxicum

Vincetoxicum hirundinaria   **Lvs** to 10 cm

Fl 5 mm diam

Lf stk 1 cm

Perennial herb to 1.2 m. Lvs broadly oval. Infl both axillary and terminal has 6–10 fls on long stks. *D:* T (not UK); *Fl:* 6–9

Bedstraw family Rubiaceae

Herbs or woody plants with unlobed, small whorled leaves. Small densely grouped flowers have parts in fours or fives, tiny or no sepals, petals in a tube and inferior ovaries.

Wild madder

Rubia peregrina

Fr
succ

Robust evergreen, stem 4-angled, down-pointed prickles; lvs leathery, prickly. *Ht*: 1 m; *D*: S, W; *Fl*: 6–8

Woodruff

Galium odoratum

Lvs
6 per
whorl

Creeping per, rhizomatous; erect shs to 45 cm. Prickles at lf edges point forwards. Long ptl tube equals ptl lobes. *D*: T; *Fl*: 5–6

Squinancywort

Asperula cynanchica

Stem
4-angled

Delicate trailing per to 40 cm; lvs linear, 4 per whorl, fls 6 mm. *D*: T; *Fl*: 6–8

Hedge bedstraw

Galium mollugo

Lvs broad,
6–8
whorl

Stout per to 1.2 m. Prickles at lf edge point forwards. Infl large, dense. *D*: T; *Fl*: 6–9

Lady's bedstraw

G. verum

Mat-forming, erect shs to 1 m; lvs fine, 2 cm, 8–12 per whorl, fls 3 mm. *D*: T; *Fl*: 7–8

Blue woodruff

A. arvensis

Plant
uprt

Leaves 6–9 per whorl; fls 4 mm, hry bracts longer than fls. *Ht*: 20 cm; *D*: T; *Fl*: 4–6

Heath bedstraw

G. saxatile

Lvs 6–8
per whorl

Prostrate with fl shs to 20 cm. Prickles at lf edges point forwards. *D*: W, WC; *Fl*: 6–8

Crosswort

Cruciata laevipes

Fls in
lf axils

Stems hry

Scrambles to 70 cm.
Lvs 4 per whorl, hry,
broad, 3-veined. *D:* W,
S, C; *Fl:* 5–6

Slender bedstraw

Galium pumilum

Infl loose,
terminal

Low shs to 30 cm, few
prickles pointing back-
wards; fls long-stkd.
D: W, C; *Fl:* 6–7

Northern bedstraw

G. boreale

Lvs
to 4 cm

Erect, stiff shs to
45 cm. Lvs 3-veined, 4
per whorl; loose infl.
D: T; *Fl:* 7–8

Common cleavers

G. aparine

Fl 2 mm

Very prickly; fls on
axillary stks have
whorls of bracts. *Ht:*
1 m; *D:* T; *Fl:* 6–8

False cleavers

G. spurium

As *G. aparine* but fls
1 mm, only 2 bracts on
fl stk, lvs narrow. *Ht:*
1 m; *D:* T; *Fl:* 7

Marsh bedstraw

G. palustre

Lvs 4–6
per whorl

Delicate, scrambling to
1.2 m. Lvs blunt-
tipped; infl spread,
loose, v branched. *D:*
T; *Fl:* 6–7

Field madder

Sherardia arvensis

Ptl tube slim
to 5 mm

Prostrate shs to 40 cm. Terminal infl has many
bracts, spls evident, esp in fr. *D:* T; *Fl:* 5–10

Jacob's ladder family Polemoniaceae

Symmetrical-flowered herbs. The 5-lobed sepal and petal tubes and 5 stamens lie above the 3-stigma ovary.

Jacob's ladder

Polemonium caeruleum

Lvs to 40 cm

Erect lfy shs from rhizome. Lvs pinnate, 6–12 lft prs. Fls to 3 cm diam, v short ptl tube, stamens fill fl mouth. *Ht:* 60 cm; *D:* N, C; *Fl:* 6–7

Convolvulus family Convolvulaceae

Climbers with a milky sap. Flowers have 5 petals in a funnel and 5 free sepals. The stamens join the petal tube.

Field bindweed	Common dodder	Greater dodder
Convolvulus arvensis	*Cuscuta epithymum*	*C. europaea*

Climbs anticlockwise to 75 cm. Fls 2 cm, fl stk has 2 bracts well below spls. Lvs 4 cm. *D:* T; *Fl:* 6–9

Parasite on heather, gorse; lvs are scales, shs red; styles longer than ovary. *Ht:* 1 m; *D:* T (not far N); *Fl:* 7–9

Parasite on hops and nettles. Stems robust, styles shorter than ovary. *Ht:* 1 m; *D:* T (not far N); *Fl:* 8–9

Hedge bindweed   ## Sea bindweed

Calystegia sepium   ### *Calystegia soldanella*

Lvs to 15 cm

Fl to 5 cm

Climber. Fls 6 cm, swollen bracts longer than and enclosing spls. *Ht:* 2 m; *D:* T (not far N); *Fl:* 7–9

Prostrate shs to 60 cm. Lvs 3 cm, long-stkd, kidney-shaped; bracts smaller than spls. *D:* W; *Fl:* 6–8

105

Borage family Boraginaceae

Coarse-haired herbs. The coiled inflorescence has the oldest flowers below. Tubular pink or blue flowers have 5 joined petals and sepals, one style and a 4-lobed ovary.

Common comfrey

Symphytum officinale

Erect, much branched per to 1.2 m. Lf bases form wings down stem, lower lvs largest, to 25 cm; fr 4 black nutlets. *D:* T; *Fl:* 5–6

Fl to 1.7 cm

Tuberous comfrey

S. tuberosum

Swollen tuberous rts, stems to 50 cm, little branched; lower lvs to 14 cm, smaller than middle ones, no wings. *D:* W, C, S; *Fl:* 6–7

Hound's tongue

Cynoglossum officinale

Fl 1 cm diam

Softly hry greyish bi to 90 cm. Fr covered with barbed spines all equal length. *D:* T (not far N); *Fl:* 6–8

Green hound's tongue

C. germanicum

Like *C. officinale* but greener, hrs rougher; lvs near-hrlss above, outer fr spines longer than inner. *Ht:* 60 cm; *D:* W, C; *Fl:* 5–7

Green alkanet

Petaglottis sempervirens

Lvs to 30 cm, lower ones stkd

Coarse-hrd per to 1 m. Long-stkd infls in lf axils. Fl 1 cm has white scales in mouth of ptl tube. *D:* SW; *Fl:* 5–6

Borage

Borago officinalis

Lvs to 20 cm, lower ones stkd

Robust ann to 60 cm Fls 2 cm diam on long stks to 4 cm, stamens protruding, purple. *D:* C, S; *Fl:* 6–8

Nonea

Nonea pulla

Erect ann or per to
50 cm. Fls to 1.5 cm,
ptl tube 2 × spls. *D:* E,
EC; *Fl:* 4–5

Alkanet

Anchusa officinalis

Erect v branched per to
80 cm. Infl dense, stms
not protruding. *D:* C,
S; *Fl:* 6–8

Bugloss

A. arvensis

Bristly uprt ann to
60 cm. Lvs wavy at
edges; ptl tube just
curved. *D:* T; *Fl:* 5–9

Common gromwell

Lithospermum officinale

Ptls
to 4 mm
diam

Plant roughly hry

Much branched per to 80 cm. Lvs have obvious
side nerves. Nuts white, glossy. *D:* T; *Fl:* 6–7

Purple gromwell

Buglossoides
purpurocaeruleum

Creeping per, uprt fl
shs to 60 cm. Ptls
1.5 cm, 2 × spl length.
D: S, C; *Fl:* 5–6

Corn gromwell

B. arvensis

Fl to
4 mm
diam

Stems
little
branched

Erect ann to 50 cm. Lvs
have no obvious side
veins; nut brown,
warty. *D:* T; *Fl:* 5–7

Lungwort

Pulmonaria officinalis

Short-hrd per to 30 cm. Fl 1 cm, tufts of hrs
alternate with stamens. *D:* C, S, W; *Fl:* 3–5

Tufted forgetmenot

Myosotis laxa

Has flattened hrs on lvs, spls and rounded stems. Fl 4 mm. *Ht:* 30 cm; *D:* T; *Fl:* 5–8

Wood forgetmenot

M. sylvatica

Erect per to 45 cm, spread hrs on lvs and stems, curled hrs on spls. Fr stks 2 × spls. *D:* T (not N); *Fl:* 5–9

Early forgetmenot

M. ramosissima

 Fl 2 mm

Delicate, has spread hrs. *M. discolor* sim, but fls yellow. *Ht:* 25 cm; *D:* T (not N); *Fl:* 4–6

Field forgetmenot

M. arvensis

Plant uprt

Spread hrs on lvs and spls. Fr stks 2 × spl length; fls 5 mm. *Ht:* 20 cm; *D:* T; *Fl:* 4–9

Creeping forgetmenot

M. secunda

Hairs on stem spread, on spls flat. Fr stks 3–5 × spl length. *Ht:* 45 cm; *D:* W; *Fl:* 5–8

Marsh forgetmenot

M. scorpioides

Flat hrs on lvs and spls. Stems ridged; fr stks 2 × spls. *Ht:* 30 cm; *D:* C, N; *Fl:* 5–9

Bur forgetmenot

Lappula squarrosa

Fl 4 mm

Lvs to 7 cm, unstkd

Delicate bristly ann, erect shs to 70 cm. Fr has 2 rows of hooked spines. *D:* T (not NW); *Fl:* 6–7

Madwort

Asperugo procumbens

Lvs to 7 cm

Coarsely hry trailing ann. Spls. enlarge into 2-lipped fr covering. *Ht:* 45 cm; *D:* N, C, E; *Fl:* 5–7

Oyster plant

Mertensia maritima
 Fl 6 mm

Lvs in 2 rows

Straggling hrlss succ per to 60 cm, fl stks to 1 cm, stamens just protruding. *D:* NW; *Fl:* 6–8

Navelwort

Omphalodes scorpioides

Lvs to 4 cm

Straggles to 40 cm. Fls to 4 mm sol in lf axils, obvious lobes at ptl tube mouth. *D:* C, E; *Fl:* 4–5

Viper's bugloss

Echium vulgare

Lvs *have strong centre veins*

Roughly hry. Ptl tube lobes unequal, 4 protruding stamens. *Ht:* 65 cm; *D:* T; *Fl:* 6–9

Vervain family Verbenaceae

Plants whose flowers have 5 sepals in a tube, 5 petals, often in a two-lipped tube and usually 4 stamens.

Vervain

Verbena officinalis

Fl 4 mm

Lvs to 8 cm

Plant *often coarsely hry*

Stiff, erect woody per. Lvs pinnate, lobed. Infl a delicate spike at apex, spl tube ribbed. Fr 4 nutlets. *Ht:* 45 cm; *D:* T (not N); *Fl:* 7–9

Water starwort family Callitrichaceae

Slender aquatics with simple leaves. Separate male and female flowers on the same plant have no sepals or petals.

Water starwort

Callitriche stagnalis

♀ fl has 2 styles

Submerged lvs narrow, floating lvs spathulate in rosette. Stems to 60 cm, fr 2 mm, strongly keeled; ♂ fl has 1 stamen. *D:* T; *Fl:* 5–9

Mint family Labiatae

Square-stemmed herbs with opposite leaves. Flowers in axillary whorls have two-lipped petal and sepal tubes (the sepal tube 5 lobed, the petal tube three-lobed below) and 4 stamens.

White dead nettle

Lamium album

Rhizomatous per; uprt hry stems to 60 cm. Fls 2 cm have ring of hrs near ptl tube base. *D:* T; *Fl:* 5–12

Henbit dead nettle

L. amplexicaule

Fl
1.5 cm

Lvs
to 2 cm

Annual, lvs round, long-stkd, bracts not stkd; spread white hrs on spl tube. *Ht:* 15 cm; *D:* T; *Fl:* 4–8

Red dead nettle

L. purpureum

Lvs
round
to 5 cm

Fl 1 cm

Bushy ann to 45 cm. Lvs and bracts stkd; ring of hrs nr ptl base. *D:* T; *Fl:* 3–10

Spotted dead nettle

L. maculatum

Creeping, uprt shs to 40 cm. Lvs have pale patch. Fls 2 cm, ring of hrs in ptl tube. *D:* S, C; *Fl:* 5–10

Common hemp nettle

Galeopsis tetrahit

Straggling coarsely hry ann to 1 m. Fls to 2 cm, white, pink or purple, ptls often spotted. *D:* T; *Fl:* 7–9

Red hemp nettle

G. angustifolia

Lvs have
few teeth

Hairy ann to 80 cm, lvs to 8 cm narrow. Fls to 2.5 cm, ptl tube far longer than spls. *D:* W, S, C; *Fl:* 7–10

Large-flowered hemp nettle

Galeopsis speciosa

Flowers to 3 cm vary in col but always have some yellow; ptl tube 2× spls. *Ht:* 1 m; *D:* T; *Fl:* 7–9

Downy woundwort

S. germanica

Dense long white hrs give greyish look. Lvs narrow, blades to 1.2 cm, fls in dense whorls. *Ht:* 60 cm; *D:* S, W, C; *Fl:* 7–8

Hedge woundwort

Stachys sylvatica

Green rhizomes. Uprt shs to 1 m; lvs 9 cm oval, all stkd; fls 1.4 cm. *D:* T; *Fl:* 7–8

Limestone woundwort

S. alpina

Leaf stks 10 cm, lvs to 1.6 cm; spls equal bracteoles. *Ht:* 1 m; *D:* S, W, C; *Fl:* 6–8

Yellow woundwort

S. recta

Field woundwort

S. arvensis   *Fl* 7 mm

Delicate, branched, hry ann. Fl whorls spaced. *Ht:* 20 cm; *D:* S, W, C; *Fl:* 4–11

Marsh woundwort

S. palustris

Has rhizome. Lvs to 1.2 cm, lf stks v short; fls 1.5 cm. *Ht:* 80 cm; *D:* T; *Fl:* 7–9

Fl to 2 cm

Sweetly aromatic per to 1 m. Fls large in long slim spikes. V variable. *D:* S, C; *Fl:* 6–9

Bugle

Ajuga reptans

Has stolons; lvs in basal rosette hry on opp faces; top ptl lip short. *Ht:* 20 cm; *D:* T (not far N); *Fl:* 5–7

Blue bugle

A. genevensis

Erect shs to 30 cm. Lf blades hry, long-stkd; fls appear after basal lvs have died. *D:* T (not N); *Fl:* 5–7

Ground pine

A. chamaepitys

Aromatic hry ann; lvs cut into 3 narrow lobes. Paired fls shorter than lvs. *Ht:* 10 cm; *D:* T (not N); *Fl:* 5–9

Motherwort

Leonurus cardiaca

Lf blades to 1.2 cm

Leaf blades palmately 5–7 lobed. Ptl tube shorter than spls. *Ht:* 1 m; *D:* T (not far N); *Fl:* 7–9

Gypsywort

Lycopus europaeus

Leaves elliptic, deeply toothed. Fls 3 mm, dense whorls, only 2 stms. *Ht:* 80 cm; *D:* T; *Fl:* 6–9

Watermint

Mentha aquatica

Smells of mint. Infl dense, terminal, ptl tube 4 equal lobes. *Ht:* 70 cm; *D:* T (not far N); *Fl:* 7–10

Cornmint

M. arvensis

No strong smell. Fls in dense whorls in axils of bracts, spl tube hry. *Ht:* 45 cm; *D:* T; *Fl:* 5–10

Spearmint

M. spicata

Strong smelling per to 90 cm. Stem hrlss, branched, lvs unstkd to 9 cm; fl whorls in dense spike, spl tube hrlss. *D: T; Fl: 8–9*

Catmint

Nepeta cataria

Strong smelling herb to 1 m. Inflorescence dense, terminal, ptl tube bent half way down. *D: S, E; Fl: 7–9*

Common calamint

Calamintha sylvatica

Fl to 2.2 cm

Has creeping rhizome. Uprt shs to 60 cm, lvs round, serrate; fls stkd in loose clusters in lf axils. *D: S, W; Fl: 8–9*

Marjoram

Origanum vulgare

Lvs to 4 cm

Aromatic. Stems uprt, branched; fls 7 mm in dense head, protruding stamens. *Ht:* 60 cm; *D:* T; *Fl:* 7–9

Large wild thyme

T. pulegioides

Like *T. serpyllum* but stems square, hry at angles. Infl long. *Ht:* 20 cm; *D:* T; *Fl:* 7–8

Wild thyme

Thymus serpyllum

Plant woody, aromatic

Flower stks round, evenly spaced hrs. Spl tube 2-lipped, top lip 3-lobed. *Ht:* 20 cm; *D:* N; *Fl:* 7–8

Wild thyme

T. praecox (= drucei)

As *T. serpyllum* but stems square, hry on opp faces. Infl short. *Ht:* 10 cm; *D:* S, W, C; *Fl:* 5–8

Wild basil

Clinopodium vulgare

Hairy per. Lvs just toothed; fls in dense terminal and axillary whorls. *Ht:* 60 cm; *D:* T; *Fl:* 7–9

Basil thyme

Acinos arvensis *Fl to 1 cm*

Lvs to 1.5 cm

Branched hry ann; straggles to 20 cm. Fls in axillary whorls of 3–8. *D:* T (not far N); *Fl:* 5–9

Meadow clary

Salvia pratensis

Lvs to 15 cm

Aromatic per to 1 m; hooded fls to 2.5 cm, 2 stamens, long style. *D:* T (not N); *Fl:* 6–7

Wild sage

S. nemorosa *Fl to 1.2 cm*

Stem lvs unstkd

Stems to 60 cm have flat hrs; fl bracts longer than spl tube. *D:* C, S, E; *Fl:* 6–8

Wild clary

S. verbenaca *Fl to 1.5 cm*

Basal lvs broad; fl has white spots on lower lip. *Ht:* 60 cm; *D:* S, W; *Fl:* 5–8

Wood sage

Teucrium scorodonia *Fl 1.3 cm*

Flowers in whorled terminal spike, no upper lip as all *Teucrium* spp. *Ht:* 20 cm; *D:* S, W, C; *Fl:* 7–9

Mountain germander

T. montanum

Lvs to 3 cm, hry below

Patch-forming shrub; prostrate stems 25 cm. Fls in terminal gp, bracts lf-like. *D:* C, S; *Fl:* 5–8

Wall germander

Teucrium chamaedrys

Lvs
shiny
to 3 cm

Tufted per to 30 cm. Lvs scalloped, fls in axils of lfy bracts. *D:* S, C; *Fl:* 7–9

Water germander

T. scordium

Serrate, unstkd lvs. Fls in axils of lfy bracts. *Ht:* 45 cm; *D:* T (not N); *Fl:* 7–10

Lvs to 5 cm

Cut-leaved germander

T. botrys

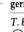

Fl to 1.4 cm

Leaves and bracts pinnately lobed, segs narrow. *Ht:* to 30 cm; *D:* S, W, C; *Fl:* 7–9

Skull cap

Scutellaria galericulata

Fl to 2 cm

Lvs to 5 cm

Hairy per to 50 cm. Lvs indented at edges. Fls in bract axils, infl 1-sided. *D:* T; *Fl:* 6–9

Lesser skull cap

S. minor

Like *S. galericulata* but to 15 cm, lvs unlobed to 3 cm, fls to 1 cm, spotted. *D:* W; *Fl:* 7–10

Dracocephalum

Dracocephalum ruyschiana

Lvs to 7 cm

Near-hrlss per. Lvs linear; fls in dense spike with linear bracts. *Ht:* 50 cm; *D:* N, C; *Fl:* 7–8

Black horehound

Ballota nigra

Stems v branched

Fetid per to 1 m. Lvs to 4 cm; fls in dense whorls with big bracts, spl teeth bristly. *D:* T (not N); *Fl:* 6–10

115

White horehound

Marrubium vulgare

Woolly v branched per. Lf blades blunt-toothed to 4 cm. Many fls in whorls. *D:* T (not N); *Fl:* 6–11

Self heal

Prunella vulgaris

Lvs to 5 cm

Stems and oval lvs often purplish, spl tube 2-lipped. *Ht:* 20 cm; *D:* T; *Fl:* 6–9

Cut-leaved self heal

P. laciniata

Like *P. vulgaris* but hairier leaves deeply lobed. *Ht:* 20 cm; *D:* S, W, C; *Fl:* 6–8

Bastard balm

Melittis melissophyllum

Lf blades to 8 cm

Aromatic hry per to 50 cm. Fls to 4 cm, spl tube 2-lipped, lower lip 2-lobed. *D:* W, C, S; *Fl:* 5–7

Yellow archangel

Lamiastrum galeobdolon

Has stolons. Leaves serrate. Fl 2 cm, top lip hooded. *Ht:* 40 cm; *D:* T; *Fl:* 5–6

Betony

Stachys officinalis

Lf stk to 7 cm

Long-stkd lvs, edges scalloped, in basal rosette. *Ht:* 45 cm; *D:* T (not far N); *Fl:* 6–9

Ground ivy

Glechoma hederacea

Fl to 2 cm

Stems creeping, erect fl shs to 30 cm, lvs kidney-shaped; few fls in whorl. *D:* T; *Fl:* 3–5

Nightshade family Solanaceae

Alternate-leaved herbs and shrubs. Tubular symmetrical flowers are 5-lobed with stamens joining the petal tube.

Woody nightshade

Solanum dulcamara

Lvs to 8 cm

Fl
1 cm

Scrambles to 2 m; lvs lobed at base. Ptl lobes 3–4 × spls. *D:* T (not far N); *Fl:* 6–9

Deadly nightshade

Atropa belladonna

Plant v poisonous

Leaf blade narrows into stk; fls drooping, bell-shaped. *Ht:* 1 m; *D:* S, W, C; *Fl:* 6–8

Black nightshade

S. nigrum
Infl
5–10 fls

Leaf blade narrows into stk. Ptl lobes 2 × spls. *Ht:* 45 cm; *D:* T (not far N); *Fl:* 7–9

Hairy nightshade

S. luteum

Fl to
1.3 cm

Stickily hry ann to 50 cm. Lvs angular-oval; infl 3–5 fls. *D:* S, C; *Fl:* 6–9

Henbane

Hyoscyamus niger
Lvs
to 20 cm,
toothed

Plant v poisonous

Fetid, stickily hry. Fls 2 cm, funnel-shaped, rigid spines on spls. *Ht:* 60 cm; *D:* T; *Fl:* 6–8

Thorn apple

Datura stramonium

Fl to 8 cm

Plant v poisonous

Stems bifurcating to 1 m. Fls sol, spls long, tubular; fr spiny. *D:* T (not far N); *Fl:* 7–10

Figwort family Scrophulariaceae

Herbs, some of them partially parasitic. Two-lipped asymmetrical flowers have 5 petals and sepals joined at least at their base and usually 4 stamens (but sometimes 5 or 2). The ovary is two-celled and superior, the fruit is usually a capsule.

Great mullein

Verbascum thapsus

Fl to 3 cm, hry stamens

Stem lvs run into stem

Robust bi to 2 m, dense woolly covering. Fls in tall dense spike, 5 stamens as all *Verbascum* spp. *D:* T (not far N); *Fl:* 6–8

Orange mullein

V. phlomoides

Lvs to 30 cm

Fl to 5 cm

Stem lvs do not run down stem at junction. Ptls hry on outside. *Ht:* 1 m; *D:* T (not N, UK); *Fl:* 6–8

Dark mullein

V. nigrum

Fl 2 cm

Lvs long-stkd

Ridged stems to 1.2 m, star-shaped hrs. Hrs on stamens purple. *D:* T (not N); *Fl:* 6–10

Hoary mullein

V. pulverulentum

Fl 2 cm

Has easily detached white woolly covering. Stamen hrs white. *Ht:* 1 m; *D:* W, S; *Fl:* 7–8

Moth mullein

V. blattaria

Fl 2.5 cm

Leaves hrlss; 1 fl per bract in infl; stamen hrs purple. *Ht:* 80 cm; *D:* S, C; *Fl:* 6–10

118

White mullein

Verbascum lychnitis

Ridged stems to 1.5 m, short star-shaped hrs. Lvs hrlss above. *D:* S, C; *Fl:* 7–8

Germander speedwell

Veronica chamaedrys

Stems to 40 cm, rooting prostrate, with 2 lines of hrs. Infl loose from lf axils, fls 2 stamens as all *Veronica* spp. *D:* T; *Fl:* 3–7

Large speedwell

V. austriaca

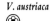

Erect per to 1 m. Infl axillary, 5 spl lobes (1 may be small). *D:* T (not N); *Fl:* 6–8

Common field speedwell

V. persica

Much branched ann to 40 cm, stems hry. Fls to 1.2 cm, sol in lf axils. Lvs to 3 cm shorter than fl stks; fr lobes diverge. *D:* T; *Fl:* 1–12

Ivy-leaved speedwell

V. hederifolia

Prostrate ann, hry stems to 60 cm. Lvs to 1.5 cm, prominent lobes. Fls sol in lf axils, stks shorter than lvs. *D:* T; *Fl:* 3–8

Heath speedwell

V. officinalis

Infl dense

Prostrate perennial, hry stems to 40 cm; infl in lf axils, 15–25 fls. *D:* T; *Fl:* 5–8

Spiked speedwell

Veronica spicata

Fl tube long

Infl a terminal spike

Hairy per to 60 cm. Lower lvs oval, top lvs linear; infl dense. *D:* T (not W); *Fl:* 7–9

Wall speedwell

V. arvensis

Erect to 25 cm. Lvs coarsely toothed; fl stks shorter than spls, top bracts longer than fls. *D:* T; *Fl:* 3–10

Spring speedwell

V. verna

Erect ann to 15 cm; lvs pinnate, 3–7 lobes; fl stks shorter than spls, fr broad. *D:* T (not far N, W); *Fl:* 5–6

Thyme-leaved speedwell

V. serpyllifolia

Prostrate per, creeps to 30 cm. Infl long, terminal up to 30 fls. Bracts longer than fl stks. *D:* T; *Fl:* 3–10

Water speedwell

V. anagallis-aquatica

Lvs to 12 cm

Hairless per to 30 cm. Lvs long; infl in opp prs. *D:* T (not far N); *Fl:* 6–8. *V. catenata* sim but pink fls

Rock speedwell

V. fruticans

Lvs hrlss. Infl terminal, fl stks longer than bracts. Large fl *c.* 1 cm. *Ht:* 15 cm; *D:* C mts, NW; *Fl:* 7–8

120

Brooklime

V. beccabunga

Hairless per to 60 cm. Lvs round, blunt; infls axillary in opp prs. *D:* T (not far N); *Fl:* 5–9

Marsh speedwell

V. scutellata

Lvs oval-linear

Hairless per to 50 cm; lvs serrate to 4 cm. Infls alt, loose in lf axils, fl stks 2 × bracts. *D:* T; *Fl:* 6–8

Wood speedwell

V. montana

Creeping per, uprt shs to 40 cm, hry all round; lvs stkd *c.* 1 cm. Infl axillary, 4–5 fls. *D:* W, C, S; *Fl:* 4–7

Slender speedwell

V. filiformis

Mat-forming per, shs creep to 40 cm. Lvs kidney-shaped; fls sol, long-stkd in fl axils. *D:* NW, C; *Fl:* 4–6

Eyebright

Euphrasia spp

Lvs opp

A gp of variable semi-parasitic anns; fls stklss in bract axils, 2-lipped, lower lip 3-lobed. *Ht:* 25 cm; *D:* T; *Fl:* 7–9

Fairy foxglove

Erinus alpinus

Ptl lobes spread

Tufted per to 15 cm. Lvs alt, obovate; spl tube narrow, 5-lobed, ptl tube slim, 5-lobed. *D:* C, S mts; *Fl:* 5–10

Foxglove ⊛ ⊛ ⊘ | Large yellow foxglove ⊛ ⊛

Digitalis purpurea
Infl 20–80 fls

D. grandiflora

Lvs to 30 cm

Stem winged

Erect bi to 1.5 m. Felty hrs all over. Fls to 5 cm spotted on lower part of tube. *D:* W; *Fl:* 6–9

Stems uprt to 1 m; lvs fine-toothed. Fl to 5 cm, yellow-brown network in tube. *D:* E, C; *Fl:* 6–9

Common figwort | Water figwort | Yellow figwort

Scrophularia nodosa
⊛ ◓ ∭

S. auriculata
⊛ ⊜ ∭

S. vernalis
⊘ ◓

Stems square, hrlss, no wings; lf stks wingless. Fls globular 5-lobed as all *Scrophularia* spp. *Ht:* 60 cm; *D:* T; *Fl:* 6–9

Hairless per to 1 m like *S. nodosa* but winged stems and lf stks. Lvs scalloped at edge. *D:* W; *Fl:* 6–9

Hairy bi or per to 80 cm. Lvs serrate. Infl in upper lf axils, fls flask-shaped, 7 mm. *D:* S, C; *Fl:* 4–6

Balm-leaved figwort

Scrophularia scordonia

Fl 1 cm

Grey, hry per to 1 m, stem square, no wings. Lvs serrate, oval to 10 cm. *D:* W; *Fl:* 6–8

French figwort

S. canina

Much branched per to 60 cm. Lvs pinnately lobed. Fls to 5 mm. *D:* S, C; *Fl:* 5–8

Common toadflax

Linaria vulgaris

Fl to 2.5 cm

Stem uprt, hrlss

Flowers as *Antirrhinum* (p 124) but with spur. *Ht:* 60 cm; *D:* T (not far N); *Fl:* 7–10

Pale toadflax

L. repens

Lvs whorled to 4 cm

Hairless creeping per, uprt shs to 80 cm. Fls pale, dark-veined, spur short. *D:* S, W, C; *Fl:* 6–9

Alpine toadflax

L. alpina

Fl 2 cm

Prostrate, glaucous. Lvs in whorls, fls long-spurred, 3–15 per gp. *Ht:* 20 cm; *D:* C, E; *Fl:* 6–9

Ivy-leaved toadflax

Cymbalaria muralis

Stems hrlss, trail to 80 cm. Lvs alt, round, 5-lobed, long-stkd. Fls to 1 cm, sol in lf axils, yellow patch at mouth. *D:* S, W, C; *Fl:* 5–11

123

Daisy-leaved toadflax

Anarrhinum bellidifolium

Fl to 5 mm

Plant hrlss

Basal lvs to 8 cm, oval, serrate, stem lvs v cut, 3–5 narrow segs. Infl a spike. *Ht:* 60 cm; *D:* SW; *Fl:* 3–8

Leafy lousewort

P. foliosa

Leafy per to 50 cm, shs hry. Infl dense spike of yellow fls, lfy bracts longer than fls. *D:* S, C; *Fl:* 6–8

Snapdragon

Antirrhinum majus

Woody per to 80 cm, brs from base. Infl terminal, fls to 4 cm, variable colour, no spur. *D:* SW; *Fl:* 7–9

Marsh lousewort

P. palustris

Lvs to 4 cm

Annual, 1 main uprt stem, spls 2-lipped, hry, top ptl lip has tooth on each side. *Ht:* 45 cm; *D:* T; *Fl:* 5–9

Lousewort

Pedicularis sylvatica

Lvs to 2 cm

Perennial, trails to 25 cm. Spls hrlss, not 2-lipped, no lateral teeth on top ptl lip. *D:* W, C; *Fl:* 4–7

Moor king

Pedicularis sceptrum-carolinum

Erect per. Lvs to 2 cm, most in basal rosette, few stem lvs; infl a spike, fl 3 cm. *Ht:* 60 cm; *D:* N, C; *Fl:* 7–8

Gratiola

Gratiola officinalis

Lvs opp

Hairless per, stems hollow, 4-angled; fls long-stkd, sol in lf axils. *Ht:* to 50 cm; *D:* S, C; *Fl:* 5–10

Mudwort

Limosella aquatica

Fl to 5 mm
4–5 lobed

Top lvs
elliptic

Hairless ann, prostrate stems produce rosettes of lvs to 1 cm. Fls sol in lf axils, spls longer than ptl tube. *D:* T (local); *Fl:* 6–10

Yellow rattle

Rhinanthus minor

Fl to
1.5 cm

Semi-parasitic per to 50 cm, lvs green, opp; spl tube flat, inflated in fr. A variable sp. *D:* T; *Fl:* 5–8

Red bartsia

Odontites verna

Hairy v branched ann to 50 cm. Infl dense spike, fls 1 cm, 2-lipped, no teeth on top lip. *D:* T; *Fl:* 6–8

Yellow odontites

O. lutea

Fl to
8 mm

Erect hrlss ann to 40 cm, many brs; infl loose, linear bracts; fls hry, stamens protrude. *D:* S, C; *Fl:* 7–9

Sharp-leaved fluellen

Kickxia elatine

Fl stks long, hrlss

Lvs arrow-shaped

Slim prostrate shs to 50 cm. Fls as *Linaria* (p 123), sol, axillary. *D:* S, W, C; *Fl:* 7–10

Round-leaved fluellen

K. spuria

Like *K. elatine* but hry and more robust. Lvs round, fls 1 cm, stks hry. *D:* S, W, C; *Fl:* 7–10

Common cow-wheat

M. pratense

Leaves unstkd. Fls in axils of lfy bracts, ptls 2 × spls. *Ht:* to 60 cm; *D:* T; *Fl:* 5–10

Wood cow-wheat

M. sylvaticum

Very like *M. pratense* but spl lobes spread and about same length as ptls. *Ht:* 25 cm; *D:* S mts, N; *Fl:* 6–8

Field cow-wheat

Melampyrum arvense

Top lvs toothed nr base

Hairy ann to 60 cm, lvs unstkd. Infl dense spike, bracts narrow, toothed, uprt, pink. *D:* T (not far N); *Fl:* 6–9

Crested cow-wheat

M. cristatum

Lvs to 10 cm

Little branched ann to 50 cm. Infl dense 4-angled spike, bracts toothed, curl back. *D:* T (rare in N); *Fl:* 6–9

Melampyrum

M. nemorosum

Hairy uprt ann to
50 cm. Lvs oval to 4 cm
wide; fl 2 cm, bracts
bluish-violet, infl lfy.
D: N, C; *Fl:* 6–8

Yellow bartsia

Parentucellia viscosa

Erect stickily hry ann
to 50 cm. Lvs not
lobed. Fls 2 cm, top lip
shorter than lower. *D:*
S, W; *Fl:* 6–10

Alpine bartsia

Bartsia alpina

Fl 2 cm

Lvs opp, unstkd
to 2 cm

Hairy per to 20 cm. Purple bracts in infl, top fl lip
longer than lower. *D:* S mts, N; *Fl:* 6–8

Cornish moneywort

Sibthorpia europaea

Lvs to 2 cm

Creeps to 40 cm. Lvs rounded, 5–7 lobed; fls
2 mm, sol, short-stkd in lf axils. *D:* W; *Fl:* 7–10

Monkey flower

Mimulus guttatus

Fl to 5 cm,
tube broad

Lvs opp, unstkd
to 2 cm

Perennial to 50 cm. Lvs rounded, toothed to
7 cm. Fls sol in bract axils. *D:* T; *Fl:* 7–9

Globularia family Globulariaceae

Simple-leaved perennials. Flowers in very dense heads have 5 sepals and petals, 4 stamens and a one-celled ovary.

Globularia

Globularia vulgaris

Infl c. 1 cm diam

Plant evergreen

Rosette lvs have 3 teeth at tip and narrow gradually, stem lvs unlobed, unstkd. Fls 2-lipped, lower lip 3-lobed. *Ht:* 20 cm; *D:* S, Swed; *Fl:* 4–6

Broomrape family Orobanchaceae

Parasites on plant roots and lacking green pigment. Leaves are scales, flowers two-lipped with a bent petal tube.

Greater broomrape

Orobanche rapum-genistae

Infl long

Fl to 2.5 cm

Parasite on gorse, broom. Top ptl tube lip unlobed, stamens join ptl tube, yellow stigmas. *Ht:* to 80 cm; *D:* W; *Fl:* 5–7

Knapweed broomrape

O. elatior

Infl dense

Fl 2 cm

Parasite on greater knapweed. Stigmas yellow, stms attached 5 mm above ptl tube base. *Ht:* 50 cm; *D:* T (not N); *Fl:* 6–7

Thistle broomrape

O. reticulata

Fl to 2.2 cm

Parasite on thistles. Fls v curved at base, have small black glands at edges and purple stigmas. *Ht:* 35 cm; *D:* T (not N); *Fl:* 6–8

Common broomrape

Orobanche minor

Stigmas
purple

Parasite on clover,
catsear. Ptl tube
curved. *Ht:* 35 cm; *D:*
W, S, C; *Fl:* 6–9

Purple broomrape

O. purpurea

Spike
loose

Stems
bluish

Parasite of yarrow.
Each 3 cm fl has 3
bracts. *Ht:* 30 cm; *D:* T
(not N); *Fl:* 6–7

Toothwort

Lathraea squamaria

Infl
1-sided

**Ptl
tube**
2 lipped

Parasite of hazel, elm.
Spl tube 4-lobed. *Ht:*
20 cm; *D:* T (not N);
Fl: 4–5

Butterwort family Lentibulariaceae

Insectivorous plants with sticky leaves or bladder traps. Flowers
have 5-lobed or two-lipped sepal tubes, spurred two-lipped petal
tubes, two stamens and two carpels.

Common butterwort

Pinguicula vulgaris

Fl mouth
has short
white patch

Oval lvs to 8 cm. Fl stk 10 cm, fls to
1.5 cm, lower lip v cleft, spur 6 mm.
D: N, W, C; *Fl:* 5–7

Large-flowered butterwort

P. grandiflora

Fl mouth has
long white
patch

Oval lvs to 20 cm. Fl stk 15 cm, fls
2 cm, shallow cleft in lower lip, 1 cm
spur. *D:* SW; *Fl:* 5–6

Pale butterwort

P. lusitanica

Fl delicate

Leaves to 2 cm. Fl stks 10 cm, fls to
7 mm, spur 3 mm, cylindrical,
pointed tip. *D:* W; *Fl:* 6–10

Alpine butterwort

P. alpina

Fl to 1 cm

Lvs to 2 cm

One or 2 yellow spots at fl mouth,
spur conical, downcurved, to 3 mm.
Ht: 7 cm; *D:* C, Arct; *Fl:* 5–8

Hairy butterwort

Lesser bladderwort

Pinguicula villosa

Fl to 9 mm

Utricularia minor

Fl stks to 15 cm

Fl to 8 mm

Very like *P. alpina* (p 129) but fl stks stickily hry. *Ht:* 7 cm; *D:* Fennoscand; *Fl:* 5–8

Slender stems to 25 cm have bladders, some stems green, some colourless in mud. Lvs lobed, palmate. *D:* T; *Fl:* 6–9

Greater bladderwort

U. vulgaris

Fl to 1.8 cm   *Fl stk to 20 cm*

Free-floating aquatic. Stems to 45 cm all green with bladders. Lvs pinnately cut into fine-toothed segs. *D:* T; *Fl:* 7–8

Plantain family Plantaginaceae

Herbs with leaves in basal rosettes. Tiny flowers in dense heads have petal and sepal tubes with 4 fused parts and 4 stamens joining the petal tube. The fruit is a capsule.

Ribwort plantain

Greater plantain

Plantago lanceolata

P. major

Fl head to 15 cm

Fl stk to 15 cm not furrowed

Lvs 3–5 parallel veins

Perennial. Lvs long, narrow to 15 cm. Infl head to 2 cm long on deeply furrowed stk to 40 cm. *D:* T (not far N); *Fl:* 4–8

Leaves to 15 cm long and almost as broad, narrow abruptly to long stk. *Ht:* 20 cm; *D:* T; *Fl:* 5–9

Hoary plantain

P. media

Softly hry lvs to 6 cm v short-stkd. Infl head to 6 cm on long stk to 30 cm. *D:* T; *Fl:* 5–8

Buckshorn plantain

P. coronopus

Leaves to 6 cm pinnately cut into narrow segs. Infl head to 4 cm on 5 cm stk. *Ht:* 10 cm *D:* T; *Fl:* 5–7

Branched plantain

P. arenaria

Scrambles to 30 cm. Lvs narrow, lower lvs have axillary shs; infl 1 cm. *D:* T; *Fl:* 7–8

Sea plantain

P. maritima

Infl long-stkd

Tuft of succ narrow lvs with 3–5 veins. Infl head 4 cm. *Ht:* 13 cm; *D:* T; *Fl:* 6–8

Shoreweed

Littorella uniflora

Fine lvd, has stolons. ♂, ♀ fls sep in same or diff heads. *Ht:* 7 cm; *D:* W, C; *Fl:* 6–8

Moschatel family Adoxaceae

Uppermost flower has two joined sepals, 4 petals and stamens, side flowers have three sepals, 5 petals and stamens.

Moschatel

Adoxa moschatellina

Fl stk unbranched

Infl 6 mm diam

Lvs 3 lobed, long-stkd

The only species in the family, a delicate herb to 10 cm with creeping rhizome. Infl of 5 fls has cubic form. *D:* T; *Fl:* 4–5

Honeysuckle family Caprifoliaceae

Woody or herbaceous plants with opposite leaves. Flowers have 5 petals and sepals and 5 stamens attached to the petal tube which may be two-lipped.

Honeysuckle

Lonicera periclymenum

***Fr** globular*

Perfoliate honeysuckle

L. caprifolium

As *L. periclymenum* but glaucous lf prs fused below, some fls in lf axils. *Ht:* 5 m; *D:* S, EC; *Fl:* 5–6

Twin flower

Linnaea borealis

***Lvs** 1 cm, short stkd*

Woody climber to 6 m. Fls to 5 cm in terminal infl are 2-lipped, top lip 4-lobed, lower unlobed. *D:* W, C, S; *Fl:* 6–9

Mat-forming evergreen. Fls 8 mm, nodding, fl stks delicate to 7 cm. *D:* S mts, N; *Fl:* 6–8

Valerian family Valerianaceae

Opposite-leaved herbs. Small 5-lobed funnel-shaped flowers have sepals indistinct from feathery attachment to fruit.

Common valerian

Valeriana officinalis   ***Infl** dense*

***Lvs** to 20 cm*

Erect per to 1.5 m. Lvs pinnate, lobed, basal lvs stkd. Fls 5 mm, 3 stamens. *D:* T; *Fl:* 6–8

Red valerian

Centranthus ruber

***Fls** to 1 cm*

***Lvs** 10 cm, glaucous*

Leaves oval. Fls white or red, narrow, spurred, 1 protruding stamen. *Ht:* 60 cm; *D:* S; *Fl:* 6–8

Marsh valerian	**Cornsalad**
Valeriana dioica	*Valerianella locusta*

Lvs
to 7 cm

| Has stolons. Lf blades to 3 cm, basal unlobed, stkd, upper unstkd, pinnate. ♂, ♀ parts in sep fls. *Ht:* 20 cm; *D:* W, C; *Fl:* 5–6 | Erect branched ann to 40 cm. Lvs unlobed. Fls in small dense heads surrounded by narrow bracts, spls indistinct. *D:* T; *Fl:* 4–6 |

Scabious family Dipsacaceae

Opposite-leaved herbs with dense round flower heads. Sepals are inconspicuous but each 4–5 lobed flower is surrounded by bracts. There are 2 or 4 stamens.

Field scabious	**Wood scabious**	**Devilsbit scabious**
Knautia arvensis	*K. dipsacifolia*	*Succisa pratensis*

Infl may
be ♀ only

Lvs in
basal
rosette

| Robust per to 1 m; lvs lobed, hry; infl 4 cm diam, outer fls larger than inner, bristly spls. *D:* T; *Fl:* 7–9 | Like *K. arvensis* but taller. Stem lvs not lobed, serrate. Infl 3 cm diam. *Ht:* 1.2 m; *D:* C mts; *Fl:* 6–9 | Unlobed lvs, midribs white. Infl 2 cm diam, all fls same size. Ptl tube to 7 mm. *Ht:* 80 cm; *D:* T; *Fl:* 6–10 |

133

Small scabious	**Teasel**	**Small teasel**

Scabiosa columbaria | *Dipsacus fullonum* | *D. pilosus*

Infl to 3.5 cm

Infl 6 cm

Stem lvs stkd

Basal lvs just lobed, mid lvs v lobed, top lvs finely cut; outer fls largest. *Ht:* 55 cm; *D:* T (not N); *Fl:* 7–8

Prickly bi to 2 m. Narrow stem lvs encircle stem; infl has long spiny bracts. *D:* S, W, C; *Fl:* 7–8

Weakly prickly bi, ridged stems to 1.2 m. Infl *c.* 2 cm, round, drooping in bud. *D:* W, C; *Fl:* 8

Bellflower family Campanulaceae

Herbs with a milky sap and simple, alternate leaves. Bell-shaped, symmetrical flowers have 5 stamens. The family includes the lobelias with asymmetrical two-lipped flowers.

Harebell	**Spreading bellflower**	**Clustered bellflower**

Campanula rotundifolia | *C. patula* | *C. glomerata*

Delicate hrlss per to 40 cm. Round, stkd lvs borne on prostrate shs. narrow unstkd lvs on fl shs. Fls nodding, 1.5 cm. *D:* T; *Fl:* 7–9

Rough per to 60 cm. Lower lvs short stkd. Infl much branched, bracts in middle of fl stks, fls erect, 2 cm. *D:* T; *Fl:* 7–9

Shortly hry per to 20 cm. Basal lvs long stkd. Fls uprt, unstkd in dense clusters. *D:* T (not N); *Fl:* 5–9

Bearded bellflower

C. barbata

Fl to 3 cm

Drooping fls in 1-sided infl, white hrs in ptl tube. *Ht:* 20 cm; *D:* Nwy, Alps; *Fl:* 6–8

Creeping bellflower

C. rapunculoides

Fl 3 cm, nodding

Spls spread

Basal lvs abruptly rounded at stk, stem lvs unstkd. *Ht:* 45 cm; *D:* T; *Fl:* 7–9

Giant bellflower

C. latifolia

Top lvs unstkd

Nettle-leaved bellflower

C. trachelium

Fl 1 cm

Hairy per to 1 m, stems sharply ridged. Basal lvs contracted at stk, stem lvs short-stkd; fls erect, spls not spread. *D:* T (not N); *Fl:* 7–9

Robust softly hry per to 1.2 m. Stem lvs to 20 cm, blades narrow gradually to stks; fls to 5 cm long, spls not spreading. *D:* T (not N); *Fl:* 7–8

Ivy-leaved bellflower

Wahlenbergia hederacea

Fl to 1 cm

Delicate creeping per, sprawling stems to 30 cm. Lvs ivy-shaped, long stkd. Slim fl stks to 4 cm, fls nodding. *D:* W; *Fl:* 7–8

135

Sheepsbit scabious

Jasione montana

Infl 2 cm diam

Lvs 5 cm

Plant softly hry

Small fls in dense head surrounded by short bracts. *Ht*: 35 cm; *D*: T; *Fl*: 5–8

Heath lobelia

Lobelia urens

Infl loose

Many serrate lvs to 7 cm. Ptl tube to 1.5 cm, 2-lipped. *Ht*: 45 cm; *D*: W; *Fl*: 8–9

Round-headed rampion

Phyteuma orbiculare

Infl 1.5 cm diam

Basal lvs long-stkd

Spherical infl, ptl lobes tubular below, then spread. *Ht*: 35 cm; *D*: T (not N); *Fl*: 7–8

Spiked rampion

P. spicatum

Fls c. 1 cm

Basal lvs to 5 cm

Flowers in 6 cm spike, ptl lobes spread as fl ages. *Ht*: 60 cm; *D*: T (not N); *Fl*: 7–8

Water lobelia

L. dortmanna

Fls to 2 cm

Spreads by stolons. Tuft of narrow lvs to 4 cm. Fl stems to 60 cm emerge from water. Infl loose, fls 2-lipped, nodding. *D*: N, NC; *Fl*: 7–8

Venus' looking glass

Legousia hybrida

Spls erect in fr

Lvs unstkd to 3 cm

Has stiff hrs. Lf edges wavy. Fls uprt, ovary elongate, spls 2 × ptls. *Ht*: 20 cm; *D*: W, S; *Fl*: 5–8

Large Venus' looking glass

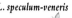

L. speculum-veneris

Fl to 2 cm diam

Much branched ann to 40 cm. Ptls as long as spls and ovary, spls spread in fr. *D*: SW, SC; *Fl*: 5–7

Daisy family Compositae

Usually herbs, but a huge and variable family. Leaves have no stipules. Small flowers (florets) are in dense heads on the flat top of the inflorescence stalk and surrounded by one or more rows of sepal-like bracts. Florets may be all alike (as thistles) or the outer ones longer (as daisies) and either tubular (disc florets) or strap-shaped (ray florets). Each ovary has one cell.

Daisy

Bellis perennis

Head to 2.5 cm

Perennial with stout rtstock. Lvs in basal rosette, serrate at tip. Fl stk 8 cm. *D:* S, W, C; *Fl:* 3–10

Pineapple mayweed

Chamomilla suaveolens (= *Matricaria matricarioides*)

Aromatic herb to 30 cm. Lvs 2–3 pinnate, fine segs. Heads have disc florets only. *D:* T; *Fl:* 6–7

Sea aster

Aster tripolium

Head to 2 cm

Lvs to 1.2 cm, lower stkd

Succulent per, hrlss lfy stems to 1 m. Outer ray florets may be absent. *D:* T; *Fl:* 7–10

Sea mayweed

M. maritima

Head to 4 cm

Lvs 2–3 pinnate, fine segs

Biennial or per, stout rtstock. Common weed *M. perforata* sim but ann. *Ht:* 50 cm; *D:* W, N; *Fl:* 7–9

137

Golden rod

Solidago virgaurea

Stem lvs toothed

Erect, few brs. Fl heads to 1 cm in terminal clusters. *Ht:* 55 cm; *D:* T; *Fl:* 7–9

Blue fleabane

Erigeron acer

Basal lvs to 7 cm

Dense, long hrs on stem and lvs. Many ray florets in 2 or more rows. *Ht:* 30 cm; *D:* T; *Fl:* 7–8

Canadian fleabane

Conyza canadensis

Stems branched to 1 m, many narrow lvs to 4 cm. Heads 4 mm, sev rows ray florets. *D:* T; *Fl:* 8–9

Gallant soldier

Galinsoga parviflora

Many brs; serrate lvs in opp prs. Oval bracts round 5-rayed heads. *Ht:* 60 cm; *D:* T (not N); *Fl:* 5–11

Ploughman's spikenard

Inula conyza

Robust bi or per, red stems to 1.3 m; heads in loose terminal gps, no rays, narrow bracts. *D:* W, S, C; *Fl:* 7–9

Fleabane

I. britannica

Erect per to 60 cm, usually v hry. Heads to 4 cm, usually sol, bracts narrow, hry. *D:* S, C; *Fl:* 7–8

Golden samphire

I. crithmoides

. *Lvs*
to 6 cm

Hairless, succ per; lvs
fleshy, 3-toothed at tip.
Heads have many ray
florets. *Ht:* 70 cm; *D:*
S; W; *Fl:* 7–8

Leopardsbane

Doronicum pardalianches

Basal lvs hry, heart-
shaped. Heads to 6 cm
single row large ray
florets. *Ht:* 60 cm; *D:*
W; *Fl:* 5–7

Elecampane

I. helenium

Head to 6 cm

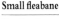

Robust per, stems rigid to 1.5 m. Basal lvs to
40 cm, stks, stem lvs densely hry below clasp shs.
Heads sol, many rays. *D:* T; *Fl:* 7–8

Common fleabane

Pulicaria dysenterica

Head
to 3 cm

Plant
perennial

Stem lvs wavy edged,
v hry below; 1 row ray
florets 2 × disc florets.
Ht: 40 cm; *D:* S, W, C;
Fl: 8–9

Small fleabane

P. vulgaris

Head 1 cm

Plant
ann, hry

Stem lvs not rounded
at base. Ray florets 1
row, no longer than
disc ones. *Ht:* 30 cm;
D: T (not N); *Fl:* 8–9

139

Corn chamomile

Anthemis arvensis

Head *to 3 cm*

Lvs *hry below*

Stems *hry*

Leaves v cut, top seg linear. Scales between disc florets. *Ht:* 40 cm; *D:* T (not far N); *Fl:* 6–7

Ox-eye daisy

Leucanthemum vulgare

Basal lvs *serrate*

Erect stems to 70 cm plus non-flowering lfy rosettes. Heads sol, long rays to 5 cm. *D:* T; *Fl:* 6–8

Coltsfoot

Tussilago farfara

Lvs *to 20 cm*

Round, toothed lvs appear after fls. All florets have strap–shaped ligule. *Ht:* 10 cm; *D:* T; *Fl:* 3–4

140

Tansy

Tanacetum vulgare

Lvs *to 25 cm*

Strong-smelling per. Lvs pinnate, lobes toothed, no ray florets. *Ht:* 80 cm; *D:* T; *Fl:* 7–9

Corn marigold

Chrysanthemum segetum

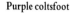

Lvs *to 8 cm*

Erect hrlss ann to 50 cm; lvs succ, coarsely toothed. Heads to 6.5 cm, sol, long-stkd. *D:* W; *Fl:* 6–8

Purple coltsfoot

Homogyne alpina

Basal lvs kidney-shaped, toothed, purple below. Heads sol to 1.5 cm. *Ht:* 20 cm; *D:* W, C, S; *Fl:* 5–8

Dandelion

Taraxacum officinale

Leaf lobes curl back; infl stk unbranched, 2 rows bracts, outer ones bent back. *Ht:* 40 cm; *D:* T; *Fl:* 3–10

Common andryala

Andryala integrifolia

Erect ann to 80 cm. Lvs to 8 cm, soft star-shaped hrs. Infl stks lfy, branched, head 1 cm. *D:* SW; *Fl:* 4–7

Smooth catsear

Hypochoeris glabra

Lvs nearly hrlss

Annual to 40 cm. The heads open only in full sun, florets just as long as bracts. *D:* T (not N); *Fl:* 6–10

Rough hawkbit

Leontodon hispidus

Head to 4 cm

Spotted catsear

H. maculata

Leaves to 15 cm, hry, spotted purple. No scale bracts on infl stk. *Ht:* 60 cm; *D:* T (not N, NW); *Fl:* 6–8

Catsear

H. radicata

Unbranched hrs on lvs; top of branched fl stk swollen, has scale bracts. *Ht:* 50 cm; *D:* T (not NE); *Fl:* 6–9

Dense forked hrs all over. Infl stk hry, no scales among florets unlike *L. autumnalis*. *Ht:* 45 cm; *D:* T; *Fl:* 6–9

141

Ragwort

Senecio jacobaea

Alpine ragwort

S. nemorensis

Head
to 2.5 cm

Erect bi or per to 1.5 m. Stem ridged, often with long hrs; basal lvs deeply lobed in rosette, stem lvs pinnate. *D:* T; *Fl:* 6–10

Robust lfy per to 2 m. Lvs toothed, hry below. Heads 3 cm, densely gpd, bracts in 1 row as most *Senecio* spp. *D:* C, S; *Fl:* 7–9

Groundsel

S. vulgaris

Oxford ragwort

S. squalidus

Broad-leaved ragwort

S. fluviatilis

Erect ann to 45 cm. Lvs lobed, clasping, may have woolly hrs. Heads to 1 cm, rarely with ray florets. *D:* T; *Fl:* 1–12. *S. sylvaticus* sim but always with rays.

Stks *of lower lvs winged*

Hairless erect ann to 30 cm. Heads to 2 cm in irregular gps have ray florets. *Ht:* 25 cm; *D:* C, S; *Fl:* 5–12

Has stolons. Uprt shs to 1.5 m. Lvs hrlss, serrate to 20 cm. Heads 3 cm have rays. *D:* C, E; *Fl:* 7–9

142

Marsh ragwort

Senecio aquaticus

No stolons; brs uprt; forward-pointed lobes on stem lvs. *Ht:* 60 cm; *D:* S, W, C; *Fl:* 7–8

Field fleawort

S. integrifolius

Basal lvs serrate, stks winged. Heads to 2.5 cm in umbel-like gps. *Ht:* 70 cm; *D:* T (local); *Fl:* 6–7

Marsh fleawort

S. congestus

Lvs *to* **12 cm**

Stems hry, uprt to 1 m. Lvs linear, hry, serrate, pointed tips, woolly bracts. *D:* C, E; *Fl:* 6–7

Hoary ragwort

S. erucifolius

Has stolons. Stem lvs hry below, top lobe pointed. *Ht:* 1 m; *D:* T (not NW); *Fl:* 7–8

Bristly ox-tongue

Picris echioides

Plant *bristly*

Head has 3–5 lfy outer bracts, all florets have ligules. *Ht:* 90 cm; *D:* S; *Fl:* 6–10

Goat's beard

Tragopogon pratensis

Linear, pointed lvs; 1 whorl bracts longer than florets. *Ht:* to 70 cm; *D:* T; *Fl:* 6–7

143

Smooth hawksbeard

Crepis capillaris

Beaked hawksbeard

C. vesicaria

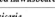

Head to 2.5 cm

Marsh hawksbeard

C. paludosa

Stem lvs arrow-shaped below; infl 1 cm, bracts not spread. *Ht:* 70 cm; *D:* W, C, S; *Fl:* 6–9

Bracts spreading. Fr beaked, pappus longer than bracts. *Ht:* 60 cm; *D:* S, C, W; *Fl:* 5–7

Erect to 90 cm. Heads to 2.5 cm, bracts hry, pappus brown bristles. *D:* N, C; *Fl:* 7–9

Orange hawkweed

Hieracium aurantiacum

Heads brown or orange-red

Has stolons. Simple hrs on lvs. Fl stks to 65 cm have dark hrs. *D:* N, C mts; *Fl:* 6–8

Leafy hawkweed

H. umbellatum

Mouse-ear hawkweed

H. pilosella

Leaf hrs sparse above, dense below. Red stripe on ligule back *Ht:* 20 cm; *D:* T; *Fl:* 5–8

Alpine hawkweed

H. alpinum

Lvs to 10 cm

Stems hry to 15 cm; lf hrs long, simple. Large heads to 3 cm. *D:* N, C; *Fl:* 7–8

Stems uprt lfy to 1 m. Crowded stem lvs to 15 cm below, smaller above. *D:* T; *Fl:* 8–9

Perennial sow thistle | ## Marsh sow thistle

Sonchus arvensis **Head** to 5 cm

S. palustris **Head** c. 4 cm

Bract hrs black, sticky

Stem sticky, hry

Robust per to 1.5 m. Round lobes on stem lvs encircle stem. Bract hrs yellow, sticky. *D:* T; *Fl:* 7–10

Ridged stems to 3 m. Lf lobes long, lance-shaped, spread, bases pointed. *D:* T (not N); *Fl:* 7–9

Smooth sow thistle | ## Prickly sow thistle | ## Scorzonera

S. oleraceus

S. asper

Scorzonera laciniata

Stems ridged

Hairless ann to 1.5 m. Lvs spiny, pointed lobes encircle stem. Heads to 2.5 cm, fr rough. *D:* T; *Fl:* 6–8

Like *S. oleraceus* but prickly lvs have round lobes encircling stem. Fr smooth. *Ht:* 1 m; *D:* T; *Fl:* 6–8

Scrambles to 60 cm; lvs pinnate, lobes narrow or round. Sev rows of bracts; fr base tubular. *D:* C, S; *Fl:* 4–7

Chicory

Cichorium intybus

Stiff per to 1.2 m.
Heads 3 cm, unstkd in
clusters of 2–3 in lf
axils. *D:* T; *Fl:* 7–10

Lamb's succory

Arnoseris minima

**Bracts
keeled**

All lvs in rosette. Infl
stks to 30 cm, very
swollen below heads.
D: W, C; *Fl:* 6–8

Nipplewort

Lapsana communis

Annual to 90 cm. Lvs
in basal rosette and on
infl stk. Heads to 2 cm
in loose gps of 15–20.
D: T; *Fl:* 7–9

Prickly lettuce

Lactuca serriola

Head
cylindrical

Stiff stems to 1.5 m;
stem lvs uprt, spiny at
edges and on white
midrib. *D:* T; *Fl:* 7–9

Blue lettuce

L. perennis

Erect per to 80 cm.
Spineless lvs have
narrow lobes. Heads to
4 cm diam cylindrical
on long stks to 8 cm.
D: C; *Fl:* 5–8

Least lettuce

L. saligna

Basal lvs
lobed

Stem lvs linear, not
spiny, lobed at base.
Heads in spike. *Ht:*
1 m; *D:* S, C; *Fl:* 7–8

Wall lettuce

Mycelis muralis

Stks *of lower lvs winged*

Erect per to 1 m. Lower lvs have big top lobe itself 3-lobed; head of 5 ligulate fls. *D:* T; *Fl:* 7–9

Globe thistle

Echinops sphaerocephalus

Plant *spiny*

Leaves pinnately lobed, hry esp below. Spherical head to 6 cm diam. *D:* S, C; *Fl:* 6–9

Lesser burdock

Arctium minus

Plant *bushy*

Bushy bi to 1.3 m. Lvs unlobed, lower lf stks hollow. Many hooked bracts in heads. *D:* T; *Fl:* 7–9

Purple lettuce

Prenanthes purpurea

Leaves elliptical, glaucous to 80 cm. Heads 2–5 narrow cylindric fls. *Ht:* 1 m; *D:* C, S mts; *Fl:* 7–9

Milk thistle

Silybum marianum   **Head** *to 5 cm*

Bracts *have big, spread spines*

Lvs *lobed*

Stems ridged, woolly, unwinged to 1.2 m. White patches on veins of spiny lvs. *D:* S, W; *Fl:* 6–8

Greater burdock

A. lappa

As *A. minus* but basal lvs broader, lf stks solid. Fls fewer, long-stkd heads 3 cm. *Ht:* 1.2 m; *D:* T (not far N); *Fl:* 7–9. *A. tomentosum* sim, cobweb-like hrs in fl head

147

Stemless carline thistle

Carlina acaulis

Lvs to 30 cm

Unstalked heads to 5 cm in centre of rosette of spiny lvs. Inner bracts silvery white, spread. Fls white to brown. *Ht:* 30 cm; *D:* S; *Fl:* 5–9

Carline thistle

Carlina vulgaris

Inner bracts ray-like

Erect bi to 60 cm. Rosette of woolly lvs in 1st year lost before 4 cm fls arise in 2nd. *D:* T; *Fl:* 7–10

Stemless thistle

C. acaule   *Head to 4 cm*

Rosette of spiny lvs to 15 cm. Sev central fl heads on v short stks. *Ht:* 20 cm; *D:* C, W, S; *Fl:* 7–9

Spear thistle

Cirsium vulgare

Basal lvs prickly, hry to 30 cm

Stems to 1.5 m, spiny wings discontinuous in broken patches. Globular heads to 5 cm. *D:* T; *Fl:* 7–10

Cabbage thistle

C. oleraceum

Head to 4 cm

Lvs elliptic, deeply cut

Stems uprt, grooved, unwinged to 1.2 m. Stem lvs unlobed, top lvs extend over heads. *D:* T; *Fl:* 7–9

Marsh thistle

Cirsium palustre

Stems continuously winged to 1.5 m, stem lvs run into wings. Heads 2 cm, purple bracts. *D:* T; *Fl:* 7–9

Creeping thistle

C. arvense

Patch-forming per to 1 m. Stems lfy, not winged. Heads may be sol. *D:* T; *Fl:* 7–9

Melancholy thistle

C. helenioides

Lvs *v hry*

Stems *woolly, unwinged*

Has stolons. Basal lf lobes point forwards, top lvs clasping. *Ht:* 1 m; *D:* N, S; *Fl:* 7–8

Woolly thistle

C. eriophorum
Head *spherical, sol to 3.5 cm*

Robust bi. Stems ridged, unwinged to 1.5 m. Basal lvs 60 cm, pinnate lobed, cottony below. Dense woolly hrs on bracts. *D:* W, C; *Fl:* 7–9

Meadow thistle

C. dissectum

Basal lvs *to 25 cm*

Like *C. helenioides* but to 80 cm, lvs less hry below, heads to 3 cm. *D:* W; *Fl:* 6–8

149

Welted thistle

Carduus acanthoides

Plant covered with cottony white hrs

Winged stems to 1.5 m, wings stop well below unstkd fl heads to 2.5 cm. *D:* T; *Fl:* 6–8

Musk thistle

C. nutans

Heads nodding to 5 cm

Stems woolly, winged except below heads. Bracts spiny, spread. *Ht:* 80 cm; *D:* W, C; *Fl:* 5–8

Winged thistle

C. crispus

Infl stks to 8 cm

As *C. acanthoides* but stems near hrlss, wings narrow. *Ht:* 1 m; *D:* T (not UK); *Fl:* 6–10

Cotton thistle

Onopordum acanthium

Head to 5 cm

Stems winged, woolly to 1.5 m. Globular heads, woolly bracts. *D:* C, S; *Fl:* 7–9

Alpine saw wort

Saussurea alpina

Lvs woolly below

Rosettes of non-spiny serrate lvs to 18 cm. Stems cottony, heads 2 cm in small gps. *Ht:* 30 cm; *D:* N, S; *Fl:* 8–9

Alpine sow thistle

Cicerbita alpina

Ridged stem to 2 m, reddish hrs above. Heads 2 cm, stickily hry in loose gps. *D:* N, S; *Fl:* 7–9

Greater knapweed

Centaurea scabiosa
Head *to 5 cm*

Stems *grooved*

Basal lvs pinnate. Outer florets big, spread. *Ht:* 70 cm; *D:* T; *Fl:* 7–9. *C. jacea* sim, brown bracts

Perennial cornflower

C. montana

Head *to 1.5 cm*

Lvs *unlobed*

Creeping, rhizomatous. Winged stems to 80 cm. Outer florets blue, inner purple. *D:* C mts; *Fl:* 5–7

Cornflower

C. cyanus

Basal lvs *to 20 cm*

Stiff, cottony stems to 90 cm. Basal lvs pinnate lobed, hry; heads to 3 cm. *D:* T; *Fl:* 6–8

Black knapweed

C. nigra

Tough, branching per, stems uprt, grooved, hry to 90 cm. Basal lvs unlobed. Heads to 4 cm diam, no spreading florets. Bracts dark at tips. *D:* W, C, S; *Fl:* 6–9

Rough star thistle

C. aspera

Erect to 90 cm. Heads sol, 2.5 cm, bracts have finger-like spines spread at tips. *D:* SW; *Fl:* 7–9

Red star thistle

C. calcitrapa

Pinnate lvs, lobes spined. Bracts spreading to 2.5 cm with 1 spine. *Ht:* 45 cm; *D:* S, W, C; *Fl:* 7–9

Saw wort

Serratula tinctoria

Head c. 2 cm

Lvs to 25 cm

Pinnate lobed lvs have
finely pointed teeth.
♂, ♀ fls separate. *Ht:*
65 cm; *D:* T (not NE);
Fl: 7–9

Hemp agrimony

Eupatorium cannabinum

Lvs to 10 cm

Robust, uprt per to 1.2 m. Lvs opp, 3-lobed,
lobes toothed. Heads in dense terminal gps each
with *c.* 6 tubular florets. *D:* T; *Fl:* 7–9

Mountain everlasting

Antennaria dioica

Heads
clustered

Lvs to
4 cm

Has stolons. Lvs in rosettes have
dense white hrs below. Bracts
dense, woolly. *Ht:* 15 cm; *D:* T;
Fl: 6–7

Common cudweed

Filago vulgaris

Lvs to 2 cm

Woolly uprt ann to 35 cm. Lvs uprt,
wavy, white hrs; 20–40 heads form
dense group. *D:* S, W, C; *Fl:* 7–8

Small cudweed

Logfia minima

Delicate ann to 15 cm; lvs to 1 cm. Heads, 3 mm, 3–6 in a cluster. *D:* T (not NE); *Fl:* 6–9

Dwarf cudweed

O. supina

Heads form short spike

Prostrate per, forms small tussocks. Lvs woolly. Fl shs to 12 cm. *D:* N, S, C; *Fl:* 7

Marsh cudweed

Filaginella uliginosa

Plant annual

Basal lvs to 5 cm

Many brs from base; 3–10 heads in dense group, v long lvs at infl bse. *Ht:* 10 cm; *D:* T; *Fl:* 7–8

Heath cudweed

Omalotheca sylvatica

Head 2 mm

Basal lvs to 8 cm. Axillary heads in loose spikes. *Ht:* 45 cm; *D:* T; *Fl:* 7–9

Helichrysum

H. arenarium

Basal lvs to 7 cm, obovate

Hairy per, stem lvs short, linear. Heads globular, bracts orange-yellow. *Ht:* 20 cm; *D:* S, C; *Fl:* 7–9

Micropus

Bombycilaena erecta

Lvs all narrow

Heads in dense terminal gps to 1 cm diam; some lvs overtop fl clusters. *Ht:* 10 cm; *D:* S, C; *Fl:* 6–7

Yarrow

Achillea millefolium

Sneezewort

A. ptarmica

Aromatic per. Stems uprt to 45 cm,
Lvs v cut. Heads *c.* 5 mm, 5-rayed in
dense clusters. *D:* T; *Fl:* 6–8

Nodding bur marigold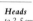

Bidens cernua

Ridged shs to 60 cm. Lvs linear,
serrate, unlobed. Heads *c.* 1.5 cm in
loose cluster. *D:* T; *Fl:* 7–8

Trifid bur marigold

B. tripartita

Bracts
*large,
fly*

Heads
to 2.5 cm

Lvs *to 15 cm*

Erect ann to 60 cm. Lvs unlobed,
unstkd. Heads to 2.5 cm, drooping,
no rays. *D:* T (not far N); *Fl:* 7–9

Many brs. Lvs to 15 cm, stkd, 3-
lobed, serrate. Heads erect. *Ht:*
45 cm; *D:* T (not far N); *Fl:* 7–9

Butterbur

Petastites hybridus

Rhizomatous per. Lvs to 90 cm. Fl shs to 40 cm. Serrate lvs appear after fl
shs. Heads in dense gps, ♂, ♀ separate. *D:* T (not N); *Fl:* 3–5

Mugwort | Field worwmood

Artemisia vulgaris

Head to 4 mm

A. campestris

Head to 4 mm

Stem has
scattered hrs

Tufted aromatic per to 1.2 m. Lvs pinnate lobed, pointed, dark and hrlss above, white, woolly below. Heads oval. *D:* T; *Fl:* 7–9

Unscented creeping per to 60 cm. Lvs v cut into narrow linear segs, hry at first then hrlss. Heads globular. *D:* T (not NW); *Fl:* 8–9

Wormwood | Sea wormwood | Cotton weed

Artemisia absinthium

A. maritima

Head
to 2 mm

Otanthus maritimus

Aromatic per to 90 cm. Like *A. vulgaris* but lf segs more rounded, silky hrs on both sides. Heads globular or bell-shaped. *D:* T; *Fl:* 7–8

Very aromatic per to 50 cm. White woolly hrs all over lvs and stems; heads drooping. *D:* W, N; *Fl:* 8–9

Woody-based per to 30 cm, stems densely woolly, white. Lvs not lobed, felty. Heads to 9 mm have felty white bracts. *D:* W; *Fl:* 8–9

155

Water plantain family Alismataceae

Aquatic or wetland herbs with unlobed, stalked, sometimes floating leaves. Flowers have three sepals and petals and 6 or 3 stamens. There are usually many free carpels.

Common water plantain

Alisma plantago-aquatica

Fl 1 cm

Lf blades oval to 20 cm

Leaves long-stkd. Infl v branched, carpels flat, 1 whorl. *Ht*: 80 cm; *D*: T (not far N); *Fl*: 6–8

Floating water plantain

Luronium natans   *Lvs 8 cm*

Slim floating shs to 50 cm. Lvs long-stkd, fls sol, long-stkd in lf axils. *D*: W, C; *Fl*: 7–8

Star-fruit

Damasonium alisma

Fl 6 mm

Stems to 30 cm; 6–10 carpels in 1 whorl make spread star when ripe. *D*: SW; *Fl*: 6–8

Parnassus-leaved water plantain

Caldesia parnassifolia

Erect per to 80 cm. Lf blades cleft at base, infl whorled. *D*: S, C, E; *Fl*: 7–9

Arrowhead

Sagittaria sagittifolia

Lf blade 15 cm

Fl 2 cm

Floating lvs oval, uprt arrow-shaped. ♂, ♀ separate, ♂ fls many stamens. *Ht*: 70 cm; *D*: T (not far N); *Fl*: 7–8

Lesser water plantain

Baldellia ranunculoides

Erect herb to 20 cm. Lf blades 3 cm. Fls 1.5 cm diam in umbel or 2 whorls, fl stks vary in length up to 10 cm; fr curved. *D*: W; *Fl*: 5–8

Flowering rush family Butomaceae
Frogbit family Hydrocharitaceae

Aquatic or wetland herbs. Flowering rushes have three-petalled and sepalled flowers in umbels and 6–9 unjoined stamens and carpels. Frogbit flowers have three petals, three or no sepals, one to many stamens and 2–5 fused carpels.

Flowering rush

Butomus umbellatus

Hairless per. Lvs long, narrow, twisted. Fls *c.* 3 cm diam in an umbel with pointed bracts.
Ht: 1 m; *D:* T (not NW); *Fl:* 7–9

Water soldier

Stratiotes aloides

Dense lfy clusters, new plants develop on stolons. Lvs stiff, spiny-toothed. Fls to 4 cm on short shs.
Ht: 40 cm; *D:* C, E; *Fl:* 6–8

Canadian pondweed

Elodea canadensis

Lvs to 1 cm

Submerged stems to 3 m. Lvs 3 per whorl have tiny teeth. Fls 5 mm. *D:* T (not N); *Fl:* 5–10

Frogbit

Hydrocharis morsus-ranae

Fl 2 cm, above water

Lf blades to 3 cm

Floating herb to 3 m; rts in bunches with lvs. Floating lvs heart-shaped. Opp pair of bracts at fl stk base. *D:* T (not N); *Fl:* 7–8

Eel grass family Zosteraceae

Marine grass-like herbs with creeping rhizomes. Flowers in dense spike are alternately male and female.

Eel grass

Zostera marina

Rhizomatous per to 60 cm. Lvs to 50 cm long by 1 cm broad, rounded at tips, sheathed at base. *Z. noltii* sim but lvs to 12 cm. *D:* T; *Fl:* 6–9

Pondweed family Potamogetonaceae

Flexible-stemmed aquatics. Floating leaves are broad, submerged ones narrow. Flowers have 4 bracts and 4 stamens.

Broad-leaved pondweed

Potamogeton natans

Spike to 8 cm

Stems to 5 m. Floating lf blades to 1.3 cm, joint at stk attachment. Lf stks winged. *D:* T; *Fl:* 5–9

Shining pondweed

P. lucens

Stems to 6 m. Submerged lvs to 20 cm, wavy edges, no floating lvs. *D:* T (not N); *Fl:* 6–9

Bog pondweed

P. polygonifolius

Spike to 4 cm

Stems to 60 cm. Floating lvs to 6 cm with large blunt stipules to 4 cm at base. *D:* W; *Fl:* 5–10

Opposite-leaved pondweed

Groenlandia densa

Lvs to 2.5 cm

Much branched stems to 30 cm; lvs in opp prs, toothed edges, all submerged. *D:* W; *Fl:* 5–9

Tasselweed family Ruppiaceae
Naiad family Najadaceae

Submerged aquatic herbs. Tasselweeds have hair-like leaves and flowers in umbels without sepals or petals. Naiads have whorled leaves and separate male and female flowers, the male with one stamen and a bract, female with 2–4 stigmas.

Beaked tasselweed
Ruppia maritima

Slender naiad
Najas flexilis

Fls in lf axils

Holly-leaved naiad
N. marina

Delicate per to 30 cm. Stems branched, lvs linear, fr strongly beaked. *D:* T; *Fl:* 7–9

Delicate ann to 30 cm. Lvs narrow, 2–3 per whorl, not toothed. *D:* T (local); *Fl:* 8–9

Submerged stiff stems to 25 cm. Lvs spiny-toothed, mostly in opp prs. *D:* C; *Fl:* 7–8

Lily family Liliaceae

A diverse family of herbs. Flowers have two whorls of three petal-like parts which may be fused or free and 6 stamens. The ovary of three fused carpels is below other flower parts.

Orange lily
Lilium bulbiferum

Martagon lily
L. martagon

Fl 4 cm diam

Ptls curl back

Leaves linear, often bulbils in axils; 1–5 fls per gp, curled ptls. *Ht:* 50 cm; *D:* C; *Fl:* 6–7

Erect stems to 1 m. Lvs linear in widely separated whorls. Fls nodding. *D:* S, C, E; *Fl:* 8–9

159

Kerry lily

Simethis planifolia

All lvs basal, linear to 45 cm. Infl loose with short bracts, infl stk to 45 cm, fl 2 cm. *Ht*: 1 m; *D*: W; *Fl*: 5–7

Snowdon lily

Lloydia serotina

Bulbous per; stems to 15 cm with 2–4 linear lvs. Fls 2 cm, 1–2 per sh, ptls veined. *D*: C, S, Wales; *Fl*: 6

May lily

Maianthemum bifolium

Stems *have stiff white hrs above*

Rhizomatous per to 20 cm. Lvs to 6 cm, heart-shaped. Infl dense, terminal, 8–15 fls with 4 ptls, 4 stamens, fr red. *D*: T; *Fl*: 5–7

St Bernard's lily

Anthericum liliago

Delicate per to 60 cm. Lvs all basal, flat, 5 mm broad. Infl terminal, fls to 5 cm divided into 6 spread segs. *D*: C; *Fl*: 5–6

Wild tulip

Tulipa sylvestris

Lvs *to 30 cm*

Fl *to 5 cm droops in bud*

Glaucous bulbous per to 60 cm; 3 basal linear lvs. Fl erect, spreading, bell-shaped. *D*: C, S; *Fl*: 4–5

Spring squill

Scilla verna

Fl to 1.5 cm

Lvs to 20 cm

Bulbous per; infl 2–5 fls, bracts longer than fl stks. *Ht:* 20 cm; *D:* W coasts; *Fl:* 4–5

Autumn squill

S. autumnalis

Fl to 1.2 cm

Leaves to 15 cm appear after fls; infl 4–20 fls no bracts. *Ht:* 20 cm; *D:* W; *Fl:* 7–9

Alpine squill

S. bifolia

Fl to 1.6 cm col varies

Usually only 2 glossy linear lvs. Infl loose 2–8 fls. *Ht:* to 20 cm; *D:* C, S; *Fl:* 3–6

Bluebell

Hyacinthoides non-scripta

Bulbous per, narrow channelled lvs. Fl stk to 50 cm, 1-sided infl droops slightly. Fl bell-shaped to 2 cm. *D:* W; *Fl:* 4–6

Lily of the valley

Convallaria majalis

Fl c. 8 mm

Lvs long-stkd

Rhizomatous per; lvs to 20 cm, elliptic. Infl 1-sided, 6–12 nodding fls. Fr a red, poisonous berry. *Ht:* 20 cm; *D:* T; *Fl:* 5–6

Fritillary

Fritillaria meleagris

Bulbous per to 50 cm; 3–6 narrow stem lvs; 1 or 2 nodding fls to 5 cm. *D:* C, W; *Fl:* 4–5

161

Ramsons

Allium ursinum

Garlic smell as all *Allium* spp; 2 broad lvs; ridged fl stk to 45 cm, no bulbils. *D:* T (not far N); *Fl:* 4–6

Round-headed leek

A. sphaerocephalon

Lvs to 60 cm

Hollow lvs; dense infl no bulbils, 2 bracts, fls short-stkd. *Ht:* 60 cm; *D:* S; *Fl:* 6–8

Field garlic

A. oleraceum

Fl bell-shaped

Lvs to 30 cm

Leaves hollow below. Infl of few fls, many bulbils and 2 bracts longer than fls. *Ht:* 60 cm; *D:* T; *Fl:* 7–8

Sand leek

A. scordoprasum

Fl bell-shaped

Lvs to 20 cm × 1 cm

Flat linear lvs have rough edges. Infl has 2 bracts shorter than few fls, many bulbils. *Ht:* 60 cm; *D:* T (not N, SW); *Fl:* 5–8

Crow garlic

A. vineale

Bulbils present

Lvs to 60 cm

Hollow lvs; stamens protrude; 1 infl bract equals fls. *Ht:* 60 cm; *D:* T (not N); *Fl:* 6–7

Wild leek

A. ampeloprasum

Lvs to 40 cm × 2 cm

Strong ridge on lf underside, infl dense, few bulbils, 1 bract soon falling. *Ht:* 1.5 m; *D:* W; *Fl:* 7–8

Chives

A. schoenoprasum

Leaves v narrow; infl dense, 2 bracts, no bulbils. *Ht:* 30 cm; *D:* T (local); *Fl:* 6–7

Plant tussocky

Fl lobes spread

Wild leek

A. scordoprasum subsp rotundum

Fls short-stkd

As *A. scordoprasum* (p. 162) but lf edges not rough or toothed. *Ht:* 30 cm; *D:* C, E; *Fl:* 6–8

German garlic

A. senescens

Stamens protrude

Fls long-stkd

Flat lvs; infl dense, stk ridged, 2 short bracts, no bulbils. *Ht:* 25 cm; *D:* SE; *Fl:* 6–7

Small grape hyacinth

Muscari botryoides

Fl 2 mm, globular

Linear lvs broader above, 2–4 per plant. Infl dense. *Ht:* 20 cm; *D:* S, C; *Fl:* 3–5

Grape hyacinth

M. neglectum

Fl 4 mm

Leaves fine to 3 mm broad, 3–5 per plant. Infl long, dense, fls short-stkd. *Ht:* 17 cm; *D:* SW; *Fl:* 4–5

Tassel hyacinth

M. comosum

Leaves 1 cm broad; infl loose fl stks v long, fls erect. *Ht:* 35 cm; *D:* S, C; *Fl:* 4–7

Meadow saffron

Colchicum autumnale

Linear lvs appear in spring, long-tubed fls in autumn. *Ht:* 25 cm; *D:* S, C; *Fl:* 8–10

Spiked star of Bethlehem

O. pyrenaicum

Linear lvs to 60 cm; infl of many fls all less than 1 cm, all fl stks equal length. *Ht:* to 1 m; *D:* SW; *Fl:* 6–7

Common star of Bethlehem

Ornithogalum umbellatum

Fl to 2 cm

Lvs to 30 cm

Narrow lvs; loose infl, 5–15 fls, longest stks on lowest fls, ptls free. *Ht:* 20 cm; *D:* T (not N); *Fl:* 4–6

Yellow star of Bethlehem

Gagea lutea

Single hooded lf to 45 cm. Infl an umbel, 2–3 bracts at base, 1–5 fls. *Ht:* 45 cm; *D:* T (not N, W); *Fl:* 3–5

Drooping star of Bethlehem

O. nutans

Leaves to 60 cm channelled. Infl 1-sided, 2–12 large fls to 3 cm, stks all equal. *Ht:* 45 cm; *D:* S; *Fl:* 4–5

Gagea

G. arvensis

Two linear basal lvs; infl a loose umbel, 2 large hry bracts at base, fl stks hry, fls 3 cm diam. *Ht:* 25 cm; *D:* C, W; *Fl:* 2–4

Meadow gagea

Gagea pratensis

Bracts equal
fl stks

One v keeled basal lf;
infl 1–5 fls, 2 bracts at
base equal fl stks. *Ht:*
15 cm; *D:* E; *Fl:* 3–4

Belgian gagea

G. spathaca

Fl stks
hrlss

Has 2 v narrow basal
lvs. Infl 2–5 fls, 2
bracts. *Ht:* to 15 cm; *D:*
C, E; *Fl:* 4–5

Least gagea

G. minima

Has single v narrow
basal lf. Infl 1–7 fls with
2 basal bracts, slim fl
stks. *Ht:* to 45 cm; *D:*
E; *Fl:* 3–5

Scottish asphodel

Tofieldia pusilla

Rhizomatous herb to
20 cm; lvs 3–5 veins,
stiff, erect; infl dense, fl
stks lflss, fls 2 mm. *D:*
N. S; *Fl:* 6–8

German asphodel

T. calyculata

As *T. pusilla* but infl stk
lfy, each fl has unlobed
and 3-lobed bract.
Plant robust. *Ht:*
20 cm; *D:* C, E; *Fl:* 7–8

Bog asphodel

Narthecium ossifragum

Rhizomatous, mat-
forming. Lvs strongly
flattened as *Iris* spp
(p 168). Fl stk to 1 cm,
1 bract. *Ht:* 30 cm; *D:*
W; *Fl:* 7–9

Wild asparagus

Asparagus officinalis

Lf-like brs to 2 cm

Fl to 6 mm

Hairless herb to 1.5 m. Stems die back in winter. Brs lf-like, narrow, clustered. ♂, ♀ fls separate, 1 or 2 in lf axils. *D:* W coasts; *Fl:* 6–7

Whorled Solomon's seal

Polygonatum verticillatum

Has stout rhizome; stems v ridged, lvs linear, 3–6 per whorl. Fls 1–4 per stk. *Ht:* 60 cm; *D:* T; *Fl:* 6–7

Herb Paris

Paris quadrifolia

Lvs 4 per whorl to 12 cm

Rhizomatous, hrlss per to 40 cm. Fls 4 equal ptls and spls. Fr a black berry. *D:* T; *Fl:* 5–8

Solomon's seal

P. multiflorum

Fr black

Stems unridged to 80 cm. Lvs alt, unstkd. Fls to 1.5 cm, 2–5 per gp. *D:* T (not N); *Fl:* 5–6

Butcher's broom

Ruscus aculeatus

Fl 3 mm

Lf-like shs to 4 cm

Erect, stiff evergreen to 80 cm. Shs lf-like, leathery, sharp points. ♂, ♀ fls separate on flat shs in axil of small bract. *D:* W; *Fl:* 1–4

Daffodil family Amaryllidaceae

Bulbous herbs. Flowers surrounded by a non-green bract (spathe) have petals in two whorls, the inner ones often trumpet shaped. The ovary lies below other flower parts.

Wild daffodil

Narcissus pseudonarcissus

Fl to 6 cm

Erect glaucous lvs narrow, ridged. Fl stk to 35 cm, 2 ridges. Fl has trumpet equal in length to spread outer ptl whorl. *D:* W; *Fl:* 2–4

Summer snowflake | Spring snowflake

Leucojum aestivum | *L. vernum*

Lvs linear, 25 cm

Fl to 2.5 cm

Linear lvs; infl 3–5 fls each 1.5 cm, bract green-tipped. *Ht:* 45 cm; *D:* C; *Fl:* 4–5

Flowers sol, all ptls in 1 bell-shaped whorl, bract green at centre. *Ht:* 25 cm; *D:* C; *Fl:* 2–4

Snowdrop

Galanthus nivalis

Lvs 20 cm

Linear lvs, outer ptl whorl to 1.7 cm, 2 × length of bell-shaped inner whorl. Bract 2-lobed, green at centre. *Ht:* 20 cm; *D:* C, S, W; *Fl:* 1–3

Iris family Iridaceae

Plants with linear sheathing leaves not divided into blades and stalks. Flowers have 6 petals in two whorls joined in a tube, three stamens and one or two bracts. The ovary is inferior.

Yellow iris

Iris pseudacorus

Fls *to 10 cm diam, 2–3 per stem*

Tuberous rhizome. Infl stk flat, indiv fl stks as long as ovary. *Ht:* 1 m; *D:* T (not far N); *Fl:* 5–7

Butterfly iris

I. spuria

Fls *to 5 cm diam, 1–3 per stem*

Rhizomatous per to 60 cm. Flat part of outer ptl whorl short compared with shaft. *D:* C, S; *Fl:* 5–6

Wild iris

I. aphylla

Leaves as long or longer than infl stk. Like garden iris (*I. germanica*). *Ht:* 70 cm; *D:* EC; *Fl:* 5–6

Siberian iris

I. sibirica

Fls *6 mm diam, 2–5 per stem*

Tussocky. Infl stk 70 cm, longer than lvs. Bracts brown, outer ptls rounded at tip. *D:* C, E; *Fl:* 5–6

Stinking iris

I. foetidissima

Fl *8 cm diam*

Strong-smelling erect per to 80 cm. Lvs evergreen; infl stk ridged on 1 side, indiv fl stks 4 × ovary length, 2–3 fls per stem. *D:* W; *Fl:* 5–7

Sand crocus

Romulea columnea

⊛ ⊞ *Fl* to 1 cm

≋

Very slim lvs longer than fl stk, 2 ptl whorls similar. *Ht:* 8 cm; *D:* W; *Fl:* 3–5

Blue-eyed grass

Sisyrinchium bermudianum

Lvs *iris-like to 15 cm*

Erect per to 45 cm. Infl of 2–4 fls each 1.5 cm diam, all ptls sim. *D:* C, W; *Fl:* 7

Spring crocus

Crocus vernus

⊛ *Fl to 5 cm*

Channelled lvs, white line in groove, ptls all sim, joined below. *Ht:* 7 cm; *D:* W; *Fl:* 3–5

⊛ 〰

Gladiolus

Gladiolus illyricus

⊛ ◗◖ ◣◤

Erect, hrlss to 90 cm. Lvs to 30 cm. Infl 1-sided spike, 2 lf-like bracts at base of each 3 cm fl, ptl tube short. *D:* W; *Fl:* 6–8

Yam family Dioscoreaceae

Herbaceous or woody climbers with rhizome tubers and spirally arranged leaves. Clustered bell-shaped flowers have 6 petals, 3 or 6 stamens and an inferior three-celled ovary.

Black bryony

⊛ ◗◖

Tamus communis

Fr *a red berry*

Fl to 5 mm

Clambers to 4 m. Lvs heart-shaped to 10 cm. ♂, ♀ fls axillary on separate plants, ♂ stkd, 6 stamens, ♀ unstkd. *D:* W; *Fl:* 5–7

Orchid family Orchidaceae

Rhizomatous perennials forming close associations with root fungi. Unlobed leaves have parallel veins. Asymmetrical flowers in spikes are often large and showy. Similar sepals and petals form six flower segments: one back and two side sepals, two erect petals and one large central lip.

Lady orchid

Orchis purpurea

Infl dense

Lvs blunt

Leaves spotted. Fls have top lobes joined in helmet. Lip has 2 broad lobes. *Ht:* 30 cm; *D:* C, S; *Fl:* 5

Early purple orchid

O. mascula

Lip 3-lobed

Lvs to 20 cm

Blunt lvs, round dark blotches. Fl spur upcurved, long, thick. *Ht:* 45 cm; *D:* T (not far N); *Fl:* 4–6

Toothed orchid

O. tridentata

Fl lip spotted

Military orchid

O. militaris

Outer lip lobes shortest

Lvs blunt, no spots

Helmet grey and pink; outer fl lobes v pointed, lip lobes spread. *Ht:* 35 cm; *D:* C, S; *Fl:* 5–6

Dense globular infl. Prominent fl lip, lobes round with central tooth. *Ht:* 20 cm; *D:* E; *Fl:* 3–5

Monkey orchid

O. simia

As *O. militaris* but slim stems *c.* 20 cm. Pale helmet, white veins. Lip lobes narrow, linear, outer lobes longest. *D:* S, W; *Fl:* 5–6

Green-winged orchid

O. morio

Helmet purple, green veins. Lip short, 3-lobed, spotted, spur straight. *Ht:* 25 cm; *D:* T (not N); *Fl:* 5–6

Lvs to 9 cm

Bug orchid

O. coriophora

Narrow lvs clasp stem. Infl dense, fls fetid, purple helmet green-veined. *Ht:* to 40 cm; *D:* C (local); *Fl:* 4–6

Lvs pointed

Loose-flowered orchid

O. laxiflora

Lvs to 18 cm

Robust stems to 50 cm. Lvs narrow, pointed, lance-shaped. Fl lip has 2 big round lobes. *D:* SW; *Fl:* 5–6

Burnt orchid

O. ustulata

Spike dense, top buds dark purple, appearing burnt. Fl lip notched, spotted. *Ht:* to 20 cm; *D:* C, S; *Fl:* 5–6

Pale-flowered orchid

Orchis pallens

Lip *not spotted*

Leaves widest nr tip. Fls yellow, lip darker, 3-lobed. *Ht:* 20 cm; *D:* C, S; *Fl:* 5–6

Fly orchid

Ophrys insectifera

Side ptls narrow, brown, velvety. Lip 3-lobed, centre lobe v notched. *Ht:* 45 cm; *D:* T (not N); *Fl:* 5–7

Bog orchid

O. laxiflora subsp palustris

As *O. laxiflora* (p 171) but lip 3-lobed, centre lobe notched. *Ht:* 40 cm; *D:* SE, C; *Fl:* 5–6

Bee orchid

Ophrys apifera

Flower lip large, patterned, bee-like, curled tooth beneath, spls pink. *Ht:* 30 cm; *D:* W, S; *Fl:* 6–7

False musk orchid

Chamorchis alpina

Fls greenish

Inconspicuous; lvs long, narrow. Lip not deeply lobed unlike *Herminium* (p 174). *Ht:* 10 cm; *D:* N, S; *Fl:* 7–8

Late spider orchid

Ophrys fuciflora

As *O. apifera* but lip flatter and broader than long, flat appendage at tip. *Ht:* 25 cm; *D:* C, S; *Fl:* 6–7

Early spider orchid

Ophrys sphegodes

Spls green-yellow

As *O. fuciflora* but lip velvety, no appendage. *Ht:* to 45 cm; *D:* C, W, S; *Fl:* 4–6

Black vanilla orchid

Nigritella nigra

Lvs numerous, narrow

Ridged stem to 25 cm. Infl dense, conical, fls vanilla-scented. *D:* C, S; *Fl:* 6–8

Man orchid

Aceras anthropophorum

Lip lobes narrow

Narrow infl, fls have red margins, lip man-shaped. *Ht:* 30 cm; *D:* W, S; *Fl:* 6–7

Lizard orchid

Himantoglossum hircinum

Lvs to 6 cm

Stem purple-spotted

Fetid fls, lip to 5 cm, 3-lobed, side lobes *c.* 1 cm, centre lobe flexuous. *Ht:* 30 cm; *D:* W, S; *Fl:* 5–7

Pyramidal orchid

Anacamptis pyramidalis

Basal lvs to 15 cm, stem lvs smaller; spur long, thin. *Ht:* 35 cm; *D:* T (not N); *Fl:* 6–8

173

Frog orchid

Coeloglossum viride

Basal lvs rounded, blunt; lip oblong, tip 3-lobed, loose infl. *Ht:* 15 cm; *D:* T; *Fl:* 6–8

Lady's slipper orchid

Cypripedium calceolus

Ptls to 9 cm

Fl sol

Lvs oval

Lip shoe-like

Two spls join into bifid lobe underneath curled, inflated lip. *Ht:* 35 cm; *D:* E, C; *Fl:* 5–6

Musk orchid

Herminium monorchis

Infl delicate

Slim, inconspicuous; 3 short, spread lip lobes. *Ht:* 10 cm; *D:* T (not N); *Fl:* 6–7

White frog orchid

Pseudorchis albida

Glossy lvs; infl dense, columnar. Fls vanilla-scented, drooping, lip of 3 spread lobes. *Ht:* 20 cm; *D:* T; *Fl:* 5–7

Coralroot orchid

Corallorhiza trifida

Lip 3-lobed

No green pigment, has coral-like rhizome; scale lvs on stem; infl loose. *Ht:* to 25 cm; *D:* N, E; *Fl:* 5–8

Common spotted orchid

Dactylorhiza fuchsii

Lowest lvs oval, blunt, blotched

Lip has 3 almost equal lobes, centre lobe triangular, just largest. *Ht:* 17 cm; *D:* T (not NE); *Fl:* 6–8

Southern marsh orchid

D. majalis subsp praetermissa

Leaves unspotted. Infl dense, long bracts, lip slightly 3-lobed, spur robust. *Ht:* 45 cm; *D:* W; *Fl:* 6–8

Northern marsh orchid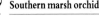

D. majalis subsp purpurella

Fls deep purple

Dense infl, purplish bracts; lip unlobed, diamond-shaped. *Ht:* 20 cm; *D:* NW; *Fl:* 6–7

Early marsh orchid

D. incarnata

Lvs to 30 cm

Hollow stems to 50 cm; infl dense, big bracts. Lip margins bend back making lip look slim. *D:* T; *Fl:* 5–7

Heath spotted orchid

D. maculata

All lvs v pointed; 3-lobed lip, middle lobe smallest. *Ht:* to 50 cm; *D:* T; *Fl:* 6–8

175

Lesser butterfly orchid

Platanthera bifolia

Fl 1.5 cm diam, spur thin

Lvs to 9 cm

Slim cylindrical infl; lip a narrow tongue, spur straight. *Ht:* 25 cm; *D:* T; *Fl:* 5–7

Greater butterfly orchid

P. chlorantha

Fl 2 cm

Loose, broad infl; lip narrow, spur long, curved. *Ht:* 30 cm; *D:* T (not far N); *Fl:* 5–7

Fragrant orchid

Gymnadenia conopsea

Lvs lance-shaped

Slim, keeled lvs; fls frag, spur long, slim, curved. *Ht:* to 40 cm; *D:* T; *Fl:* 6–8

Ghost orchid

Epipogium aphyllum

Lvs are scales

No green col; twisted fls, lip uppermost, spur vertical. *Ht:* 15 cm; *D:* C, N; *Fl:* 6–8

Bog orchid

Hammarbya paludosa

Basal lvs to 1 cm

Slender stems to 12 cm, basal lvs round, have bulbils at edge; loose infl. *D:* C, N; *Fl:* 7–9

Fen orchid

Liparis loeselii

Bulbous, lvs v glossy; fls twisted, lip wavy, point upwards. *Ht:* 15 cm; *D:* C, E; *Fl:* 7

Calypso orchid

Calypso bulbosa

Fl to 5 cm

Lip has
projections

Oval lvs *c.* 8 cm, prominent veins. Lip concave
forming a "shoe", other ptls and spls erect, lip
hry. *Ht:* 15 cm; *D:* N; *Fl:* 5–7

Birdsnest orchid

Neottia nidus-avis

No green pigment; lvs
scale-like. Loose infl,
lip large, 2-lobed at
base. *Ht:* 35 cm; *D:* T
(not N); *Fl:* 6–7

Creeping lady's tresses

Goodyera repens

Bracts
long

Has stolons, lvs oval,
stkd, net-veined in
rosettes. Fls frag. *Ht:*
20 cm; *D:* N, mts in C,
S; *Fl:* 7–8

Violet birdsnest orchid

Limodorum abortivum

Stem
robust

No green col. Hooded
fls to 4 cm, spur long,
down-pointed. *Ht:*
60 cm; *D:* T; *Fl:* 5–7

Autumn lady's tresses

Spiranthes spiralis

*Fls in
1 row*

Leaves green, scale-
like. Infl spirally
twisted. *Ht:* 15 cm; *D:*
T (not N); *Fl:* 8–9

Lesser twayblade

Listera cordata

Basal lvs in 1 opp pr, narrow at base. Lip reddish, 2-lobed, under 5 mm. *Ht:* 10 cm; *D:* N, C; *Fl:* 7–9

Common twayblade

L. ovata

Lvs to 20 cm

Basal lvs to 3 cm

Basal lvs in 1 opp pr. Lip yellow-green, 2-lobed to 1.5 cm. *Ht:* 45 cm; *D:* T; *Fl:* 6–7

Red helleborine

Cephalanthera rubra

Spls *pointed*

Lvs *pointed*

Stem stickily hry above; fl longer than bracts. *Ht:* 35 cm; *D:* T (not N, NW); *Fl:* 6–7

White helleborine

C. damasonium

Lvs to 10 cm **Lip** *constricted in centre*

Oval lvs. Fl parts much shorter than bracts; not spread, spls blunt. *Ht:* 35 cm; *D:* T (not N); *Fl:* 5–6

Narrow-leaved helleborine

C. longifolia

Fl parts *not spread*

Lvs to 20 cm

Pointed lance-shaped lvs. Most fls longer than bracts, pointed spls. *Ht:* 45 cm; *D:* C, E; *Fl:* 5–7

Marsh helleborine

Epipactis palustris

Lip *jointed*

Patch-forming with rhizome. Spls brown-purple, hry on outside. *Ht:* 30 cm; *D:* T (not N); *Fl:* 6–8

Broad-leaved helleborine

E. helleborine

Lvs *broadly oval*

Leaves spirally arranged. Fls have large round appendage over stigma. *Ht:* 65 cm; *D:* T (not N); *Fl:* 7–10

Dark red helleborine

E. atrorubens

Stem to 30 cm, dense soft hrs. Pointed lvs in opp ranks; fls red-purple all over. *D:* T (local in W); *Fl:* 6–7

Narrow-lipped helleborine

E. leptochila

Lip *red inside*

Stem *softly hry*

Leaves in 2 opposite ranks; spread fl parts shorter than lowest bracts. *Ht:* 55 cm; *D:* C, W (local); *Fl:* 6–8

Green-flowered helleborine

E. phyllanthes

Lvs *in 2 opp ranks*

Stem to 45 cm, usually hrlss. Fls droop vertically from hrlss fl stk. Lip cup white inside. *D:* W; *Fl:* 7–9

Arum family Araceae

Herbs with small flowers crowded on to a club-shaped spadix and surrounded by a bract or spathe. Male flowers are in the upper spadix, female below with 4–6 petals.

Lords and ladies, Cuckoo pint

Arum maculatum

Hairless per to 25 cm. Lvs to 20 cm with dark green midrib arise in spring. Spadix to 12 cm, half spathe length. *D:* T (not N); *Fl:* 4–5

Large cuckoo pint

A. italicum

Hairless per. Lvs to 30 cm with pale midrib arise in winter (by Dec). Spadix ⅓ × spathe, yellow tip, spathe 35 cm. *D:* W; *Fl:* 4–5

Bog arum

Calla palustris

Lf blades emergent

Aquatic per to 30 cm. Lvs heart-shaped, spathe to 7 cm, flat, 2 × spadix. *D:* C, E; *Fl:* 6–8

Sweet flag

Acorus calamus

Lvs to 1 m long, 2 cm broad

Flower stk has lateral spadix to 8 cm and continues to lfy tip. *Ht:* 1 m; *D:* T (not far N); *Fl:* 5–7

Duckweed family Lemnaceae

Floating aquatics with leaf-like or disc-shaped stems from whose undersides roots and male and female flower buds arise.

Common duckweed

Lemna minor

Floating disc to 4 mm diam, flat on both sides, 1 unbranched rt usually *c.* 4 cm. *D:* T; *Fl:* 6–7

Greater duckweed

Spirodela polyrhiza

Disc to 8 mm, reddish below. Sev rts to 3 cm arise from underside centre. *D:* T (not N); *Fl:* 7

Ivy-leaved duckweed

L. trisulca

Submerged; 3 discs held together in lobed plate to 1.2 cm. *D:* T (not far N); *Fl:* 5–7

Gibbous duckweed

L. gibba

Discs swollen, convex above and below to 5 mm; 1 unbranched rt. *D:* T (not N); *Fl:* 6–7

Rootless duckweed

Wolffia arrhiza

Disc rtlss, egg-shaped to 1 mm, rarely fls. V much smaller than *Lemna* spp. *D:* C, S

Bur-reed family Sparganiaceae
Reedmace family Typhaceae

Perennial linear-leaved aquatics. Bur-reeds have globular inflorescences of single-sexed flowers. Reedmaces have a spadix with male flowers above, female flowers lower down.

Branched bur-reed

Sparganium erectum

Lvs keeled to 1.5 cm broad

Branched infl, ♂ heads at branch tips, ♀ at bases. *Ht:* 1 m; *D:* T (not far N); *Fl:* 6–8

Reedmace

Typha latifolia

Lvs to 2 cm wide

Broad lvs. ♂ part of infl immediately over ♀. *Ht:* 2 m; *D:* T (not far N); *Fl:* 6–7

Lesser reedmace

T. angustifolia

Lvs to 5 mm wide

Narrow lvs; gap of 1–9 cm between ♂ and ♀ fls. *Ht:* 2.5 m; *D:* T (not far N); *Fl:* 6–7

Index

Entries in brackets are plants mentioned in the text but not described in full. English family names have been omitted but can be found by looking up the English names of the plants they cover. The entry 'pea', for example, will take you to the pea family.

Further reading

For more detailed descriptions consult:
Flora Europaea ed. T.G. Tutin and others (CUP)
Flora of the British Isles A.R. Clapham, T.G. Tutin and E.F. Warburg
(CUP)
Flowers of Europe O. Polunin (OUP)
Wild Flowers of Britain and Northern Europe R.G. Fitter, A. Fitter and
M. Blamey (Collins)